LooseTalk

THE BOOK OF QUOTES
From the Pages of <u>Rolling Stone</u> Magazine

Compiled by Linda Botts

Quick Fox/Rolling Stone Press

Printed in the United States of America.

International Standard Book Number: 0-8256-3168-8
Library of Congress Catalog Card Number: 80-50027

In Great Britain: Book Sales Ltd., 78 Newman Street, London W1P 3LA.

In Canada: Gage Trade Publishing, P.O. Box 5000, 164 Commander Blvd.,
          Agincourt, Ontario M1S 3C7.

Designed by Barry L.S. Mirenburg

Cover design by Werner Jurgeleit

"Loose Talk" was a regular feature of *Rolling Stone* magazine in the Seventies. It was, mostly, a collection of funny, outrageous, ironic, or downright silly statements and bloopers made by all kinds of famous and not-so-famous people; the quotes were gathered from various newspapers and magazines and from TV and radio interviews and reflected the sensibilities of the magazine—part rock journal, part political and cultural observer. In fact, one could usually find the spiciest quotes not in "Loose Talk" but in the stories and interviews in the rest of the magazine.

This book expands on the column by including quotes from the pages of every issue of *Rolling Stone* from the first in 1967 through the Seventies. We collected the funniest and most insightful for this volume. Enjoy.

THE EDITORS

FORMER PRESIDENT RICHARD M. NIXON/photo by UPI

"I don't want to be quoted,
and don't quote me that I don't want to be quoted."

CBS' WINSTON BURDETT ON THE 1948 MURDER
OF CORRESPONDENT GEORGE POLK

"I know that you believe you understand
what you think I said, but I'm not sure you realize that what you heard
is not what I meant."

RICHARD NIXON QUOTED ON A POSTER

"Society's ills come from people having lost the taste for enjoyment."

PHILIPPE JUNOT, HUSBAND OF PRINCESS CAROLINE OF MONACO

"It remains a fact that a happy person cannot be a communist."

JAMES T. KRUGER, SOUTH AFRICAN MINISTER OF JUSTICE, IN 1976

"The chief problem of the lower-income farmers is poverty."

NELSON ROCKEFELLER

"Starvation in India doesn't worry me one bit.
And it doesn't worry you, if you're honest. You just pose. You don't
even know it exists. You've just seen the charity ads. You can't pretend
to me that an ad reaches down into the depths of your soul and
actually makes you feel more for these people than, for instance,
you feel about getting a new car."

PAUL McCARTNEY

"Life is life, you know, so the new leader of Bangladesh
goes to London to have his gall bladder removed, takes over a whole
floor at Claridge's, and has an entourage of 200 people—two
private jets he flies on. His attitude is fuck those starvers.
Fuck those starvers."

ROBERT MITCHUM

"Food is a weapon. . . one of the principal tools in our negotiating kit."

EARL BUTZ, AS SECRETARY OF AGRICULTURE, IN 1975

"Sure, cancer is a long and painful illness.
But if you take the nitrites out of cured pork, you get botulism. That'll
take you out fast and you'll have nothing to worry about."

EARL BUTZ, AS SECRETARY OF AGRICULTURE, IN 1975

"Hell, there's more nitrites in a kiss than in a ton of bacon."

LARRY LEE, COMMUNICATIONS DIRECTOR OF THE
NATIONAL PORK PRODUCERS' COUNCIL

"No gasoline and no cars is bad enough.
No pasta is much worse. It's like banning espresso and girls."

NEWS VENDOR IN ROME DURING A PASTA SHORTAGE

"This lousy gas deal would make last year's
fleecing in the Russian wheat deal look like a Sunday school picnic."

REPRESENTATIVE LES ASPIN OF WISCONSIN, IN 1974, ON A PROPOSED
LOAN TO DEVELOP NATURAL GAS IN RUSSIA

"I think it is an energy crisis for consumers,
who are being subjected to billions of dollars of unarmed robbery
by the oil companies in collusion with governmental support. It is most
certainly not an energy crisis for the oil industry."

RALPH NADER

"The energy crisis has done
for big-car sales what pantyhose did for finger fucking."

A GENERAL MOTORS EXECUTIVE DURING A PRESS INTERVIEW AT A CONVENTION
OF THE NATIONAL AUTOMOBILE DEALERS' ASSOCIATION

"If it hadn't been for [my] brother
making a deal with [Libyan President Mu'ammar al] Qaddafi to leak in
all that Libyan oil, the energy crisis would have been a lot worse."

NELSON ROCKEFELLER

"By 1980 we will be self-sufficient
and will not need to rely on foreign enemies . . . uh, energy."

RICHARD NIXON, IN 1973

"We prefer economic growth to clean air."

CHARLES BARDEN, EXECUTIVE DIRECTOR OF THE
TEXAS AIR CONTROL BOARD

"The Con Ed system is in the
best shape in fifteen years and there's no problem about the summer."

CHARLES FRANK LUCE, CHAIRMAN OF NEW YORK'S CONSOLIDATED EDISON,
A FEW HOURS BEFORE THE BLACKOUT OF JULY 1977

"The use of solar energy has not been
opened up because the oil industry does not own the sun."

RALPH NADER

"When Ralph Nader tells me that he wants
my car to be cheap, ugly and slow, he's imposing a way of life on me
that I'm going to resist to the bitter end."

TIMOTHY LEARY

"The only accident is that this thing
leaked out. You could have avoided this whole thing by not saying
anything. But because of regulations, it was disclosed."

CRAIG FAUST, CONTROL-ROOM OPERATOR AT THE
THREE MILE ISLAND NUCLEAR PLANT

"In the nuclear industry . . . no acts of God can be permitted."

DR. HANNES ALFVEN, NOBEL LAUREATE IN PHYSICS

"When we think of having several thousand
reactors as we are talking about having, [we could] have a serious
accident once every three years, losing a city for example."

DR. JOHN GOFMAN, FORMER ATOMIC ENERGY COMMISSION
ASSOCIATE LAB DIRECTOR

"A nuclear power plant is infinitely safer
than eating, because 300 people choke to death on food every year."

DIXY LEE RAY, GOVERNOR OF THE STATE OF WASHINGTON, IN 1977

"I would sleep right near the nuclear plant;
there is no question about that. It is a comfortable neighbor."

JAMES R. SCHLESINGER, PRESIDENTIAL ENERGY ADVISOR, IN 1977

"The possibility of orbiting nuclear power plants
is a good one. Of course, you run into problems. People ask, 'Is it a
floating bomb?' and all that nonsense."

MIKE SMITH OF NASA'S SPACE SHUTTLE PROGRAM

"If the public knew what the facts are
and if they had to choose between nuclear reactors and candles,
they would choose candles."

RALPH NADER

"Seen one redwood, you've seen 'em all."

RONALD REAGAN ON ECOLOGY

"This Congress is in another world. It's unbelievable."

RALPH NADER ON INACTION TO RESOLVE THE GAS SHORTAGE

"I admit I may have dozed through some of the sessions.
But I haven't had a good rest since the campaign."

SENATOR S. I. HAYAKAWA ON THE HARVARD SEMINARS HE AND COLLEAGUES
ATTENDED IN 1977 TO LEARN TO BE GOOD LEGISLATORS

"Waiting for Congress to move quickly
in the right direction is like waiting for a herd of bulls
to give milk."

JOURNALIST PAUL GROWALD

"If every senator insists on knowing
what he's voting for before he votes, we're not going to get a bill
reported before Monday."

LOUISIANA SENATOR RUSSELL LONG DISCUSSING OIL DEPLETION ALLOWANCES

"It took me six months to get the chairman
of the House Armed Services Committee to start talking gibberish.
I think I've accomplished the same thing here in three months."

REPRESENTATIVE LEE ASPIN TALKING TO OTIS PIKE,
CHAIRMAN OF THE HOUSE CIA COMMITTEE, IN 1975

"When I first went to Washington,
I thought, what is li'l ol' me doing with these ninety-nine great people?
Now I ask myself, what am I doing with these ninety-nine jerks?"

SENATOR S.I. HAYAKAWA

"I must be doing something right."

SENATOR THOMAS J. McINTYRE ON BEING RATED THE WORST SENATOR
BY THE JOHN BIRCH SOCIETY

"Foreign policy is too damned important
to be left to the secretary of state."

GEORGE MEANY, PRESIDENT OF THE AFL-CIO

GEORGE MEANY/photo by UPI

"I think we need to face up to economic problems
and stop going around sucking on peppermint Lifesavers as though
that's going to help us. What needs to be drilled into the mind
of this administration is the need for W-O-R-K.
J-O-B-S—not B-S."

SENATOR HUBERT HUMPHREY

"Gun control shouldn't be put off
on the Consumer Product Safety Commission. It's up to Congress
to bite the bullet."

REPRESENTATIVE LIONEL VAN DEERLIN, CHAIRMAN OF THE
HOUSE SUBCOMMITTEE ON CONSUMER
PROTECTION AND FINANCE

"It's like having the Pope offer to make Christ a cardinal."

REPRESENTATIVE LUCIEN NEDZI, AFTER THE HOUSE OF REPRESENTATIVES
PROMOTED GEORGE WASHINGTON TO THE RANK OF
GENERAL OF THE ARMIES

"If welfare reform meant putting arsenic in children's milk,
there would be local officials who would settle for that as long as it
meant full federal funding."

SENATOR DANIEL PATRICK MOYNIHAN

"I've always felt the government really wants
to force me to hire four foot eleven transvestite morons."

LOS ANGELES POLICE CHIEF ED DAVIS, RESPONDING TO FEDERAL CHARGES
HE DOES NOT HIRE ENOUGH WOMEN OR BLACKS

"Let's hope for an epidemic of botulism."

RONALD REAGAN ON THE FOOD GIVEAWAY DEMANDED BY
THE SYMBIONESE LIBERATION ARMY

"The most revolutionary thing
you can do in this country is change your mind."

COUNTRY JOE McDONALD

"The revolution will come
from ignoring the others out of existence."

WRITER WILLIAM BURROUGHS

"I think it's inherent
within the American character to change the law
by moving outside it."

ARTHUR PENN, DIRECTOR AND PLAYWRIGHT

"Ultraliberalism today translates into a
whimpering isolationism in foreign policy, a mulish obstructionism
in domestic policy, and a pusillanimous pussyfooting on the
critical issue of law 'n' order."

SPIRO AGNEW

"The average American is just like the child
in the family. You give him some responsibility, and he is going to
amount to something. If, on the other hand, you make him
completely dependent and pamper him and cater to him
too much, you are eventually going to make him soft,
spoiled, and eventually a very
weak individual."

RICHARD NIXON

"A country that frees Ellsberg
and puts me on trial instead can't be all bad—right?"

EGIL KROGH, UNDERSECRETARY OF TRANSPORTATION, DURING THE
1974 WATERGATE TRIALS (ATTRIBUTED BY HIS WIFE)

"I didn't hear the question too clearly.
And I'm sure if you spoke it ten times, I still wouldn't hear it."

ROBERT VESCO, WHEN ASKED WHETHER HE DISCUSSED HIS CAMPAIGN
CONTRIBUTION OR PROBLEMS WITH THE SECURITIES AND EXCHANGE COMMISSION
WITH RICHARD NIXON

"I'm not saying that I bribe officials,
or anything like that. I don't bribe officials. But it doesn't hurt
to be on good terms with them, to be on the right side
of them. So you make sure the right people
get in office."

BROTHEL OWNER JOE CONFORTE ON POLITICS

"I prefer Abbie Hoffman to Richard Nixon
simply because he's more entertaining, more interesting to listen to.
I don't care what the two of them are talking about; they could
be talking about toothpaste, and Abbie's gonna come out
hands down because he's just a more entertaining guy."

GRACE SLICK

"I think the lousiest, most mediocre,
venal, grafting, lying politician in the nation is a saint compared to
the dirty bastards who sit on steps and say 'I'm in
the Weathermen' and go on an ego trip.
They're the lousy bastards."

COLUMNIST JIMMY BRESLIN

JERRY GARCIA OF THE GRATEFUL DEAD/photo by David Gahr

"We're Republicans now—real normal,
real boring guys. And it's all over, that sixties shit."

CHRIS HILLMAN OF THE REUNITED BYRDS

"It's already happened.
We're living after the fact. It's postrevolutionary age. The change is
over. The rest of it is a clean-up action."

JERRY GARCIA

"If you want to find a politician
free of any influence, you can find Adolph Hitler,
who made up his own mind."

EUGENE McCARTHY

"Don't worry, boys; we'll weather this storm of approval
and come out as hated as ever."

SAUL ALINSKY, POVERTY FIGHTER AND COMMUNITY ORGANIZER, TO HIS STAFF
IN JUNE 1972, SHORTLY BEFORE HIS DEATH

"Everybody who knows me knows I have a very poor memory."

FORMER SENATOR EDWARD GURNEY, ON TRIAL IN FLORIDA
FOR ILLEGAL CAMPAIGN ACTIVITIES

"Nobody wants to be a skunk at a garden party."

ROBERT BLOOM, ACTING COMPTROLLER OF THE CURRENCY OF THE FDIC,
EXPLAINING WHY HIS OFFICE CONCEALED BERT LANCE'S SHADY PAST

"Intelligence is a highly secretive business."

REPRESENTATIVE DALE MILFORD AT CIA HEARINGS

❦

"I think there are some things we don't want to know.
Nothing could make the Soviets happier than to see our wonderful
intelligence system destroyed."

BARRY GOLDWATER SUGGESTING THAT CONGRESSIONAL PROBES
OF THE CIA BE CALLED OFF

❦

"Mr. Walsh, please stop saying, 'I'm ignorant of those
matters.' Just say, 'That falls out of my jurisdiction.' It's much classier."

REPRESENTATIVE OTIS PIKE, CHAIRMAN OF THE HOUSE CIA COMMITTEE,
TO AN FBI REPRESENTATIVE

❦

"Well, you know how it is, nobody's human."

ALBERT HALL, ASSISTANT SECRETARY OF DEFENSE FOR INTELLIGENCE,
EXPLAINING WHY SO MANY INTELLIGENCE AGENCIES
COLLECT THE SAME INFORMATION

❦

"FBI informers share the privilege
of all Americans in their right to pay taxes, and the
Internal Revenue Service feels they should pay taxes on all their
income, including their informer fees. And so far as I know,
there is no withholding allowed for such fees."

DONALD ALEXANDER, COMMISSIONER OF THE
INTERNAL REVENUE SERVICE

❦

"It was much more exciting
being an informant than being a teller in a bank."

MARY JO COOK, EX-FBI INFORMER WHO INFILTRATED THE
VIETNAM VETERANS AGAINST THE WAR

"The biggest threat
to America today is its own federal government. . . . Will the
army protect anybody from the FBI? the CIA? the IRS? the Republican party? the Democratic party? . . . The biggest dangers
we face today don't even need to sneak past our
billion-dollar defense system . . . They issue
the contracts for them."

FRANK ZAPPA

"I believe . . . they worked without pay for the most part."

RICHARD M. BISELL, A CIA OFFICIAL, ON THE ROLE OF THE MAFIA
IN CASTRO MURDER PLOTS

"Having been raised in the hard knocks of
Detroit area life, I know the difference between a welcome mat
and a doormat."

REPRESENTATIVE LUCIEN NEDZI, OFFERING HIS RESIGNATION
AS CHAIRMAN OF THE HOUSE COMMITTEE INVESTIGATING
THE CIA

"I have lunch with my CIA escorts in the Overt cafeteria.
Covert employees eat, of course, in the Covert cafeteria, and I ask if
they pay a covert charge."

DANIEL SCHORR, DURING CBS FILMING AT THE CIA COMPOUND

"I watch all the mysteries I can.
I'm crazy about Mannix. Columbo, he's great. How do you think I
know all this stuff about the CIA?"

NELSON ROCKEFELLER

"I should think the agency
would refrain from spying on presidents."

SENATOR FRANK CHURCH ON REPORTS OF CIA INFILTRATION
OF THE WHITE HOUSE

"I think he was yielding to that human impulse of the greater good."

RICHARD HELMS EXPLAINING WHY THE CIA SCIENTIST IN CHARGE OF THE
CHEMICAL WEAPONS DIVISION DID NOT DESTROY SHELLFISH
TOXIN AS ORDERED BY PRESIDENT NIXON

"It depends on who you're talking to.
If you're talking to the head of the KGB and you happen
to be overheard, and you're Jane Fonda or somebody else, there's no
reason you shouldn't be overheard if somebody has the
capability to overhear you—which I don't know
if they do or not."

NELSON ROCKEFELLER ON ELECTRONIC SURVEILLANCE BY THE
NATIONAL SECURITY AGENCY

"The main difference I see between the old SEC and the new
one is that we [now] put in prison a much higher type of person."

WILLIAM O. DOUGLAS

"Once the toothpaste's out of the tube,
it's going to be very hard to get it back in again."

ATTRIBUTED TO H. R. HALDEMAN

"No one is entitled to the truth."

E. HOWARD HUNT, ARCHITECT OF THE WATERGATE BREAK-IN

"There are other things—animals thrashing around in the forest. I can hear them but can't see them. I do know of other things that I know should be investigated."

SENATOR HOWARD BAKER

"The Rockefeller report was the first report that was a smear and a whitewash at the same time."

JOURNALIST FRANK MANKIEWICZ, ON THE 1975 REPORT WHICH INVESTIGATED CHARGES OF ILLEGAL DOMESTIC SPYING BY THE CIA

"Anyone who thinks they acted alone must also believe in Santa Claus, the Easter Bunny, and the Tooth Fairy."

HENRY GONZALEZ, EX-CHAIRMAN OF THE HOUSE SELECT COMMITTEE ON ASSASSINATIONS

"If Moses had gone to Harvard Law School and spent three years working on the Hill, he would have written the Ten Commandments with three exceptions and a saving clause."

CHARLES MORGAN, EXECUTIVE DIRECTOR OF THE AMERICAN CIVIL LIBERTIES UNION AT A CONFERENCE

"The slowdown is gaining so much momentum it is scaring everybody."

AN ECONOMIST SPEAKING AT THE BROOKINGS INSTITUTE IN WASHINGTON

Once you have done the budget,
once you get the statistics, it is much like getting down the unvirtuous
woman. Once you get her down, you can do anything you want to."

REPRESENTATIVE RICHARD ICHORD

"Corporations are people too."

WILLIAM SIMON, SECRETARY OF THE TREASURY, PROPOSING A NEW
TAX BREAK FOR BIG BUSINESS

"I'm not saying that they should have
all the power, but I'm saying that they shouldn't have less power
than the Eagles. It's ridiculous."

LINDA RONSTADT ON THE POLITICAL POWER OF MULTINATIONAL CORPORATIONS

"Who knows who should be president
and if anybody should have a big interest in determining those things.
Shouldn't Standard Oil? I mean, they have more to gain
and more to lose."

LINDA RONSTADT

"I think we ought to sue
ol' Nelson Rockefeller for nonsupport."

FRED HARRIS, 1976 PRESIDENTIAL CANDIDATE, ON
TAX BREAKS FOR BIG BUSINESS

"I'm afraid to say anything anymore.
Whatever I say, someone wants to blame the U.S. government for it."

ANDREW YOUNG, UN AMBASSADOR

"All government bothers my conscience."

GOVERNOR JERRY BROWN

"The worst thing to look like
right now is a politician; this is a bad year for them."

FRANK MANKIEWICZ, APRIL 1972, THEN
PRESIDENTIAL CAMPAIGN DIRECTOR FOR GEORGE McGOVERN

"What I'd like to have him do
is get to the top of the slope and push Ron Nessen down."

FORD CAMPAIGN MANAGER HOWARD CALLAWAY ON THE
PRESIDENT'S NEW HAMPSHIRE CAMPAIGN

"I see Plains going straight to hell."

BILLY CARTER AFTER HIS UNSUCCESSFUL BID FOR MAYOR

"Most politicians have a right
to feel morally superior to their constituencies."

SENATOR DANIEL PATRICK MOYNIHAN

"I'll never run for anything. . . . God, you
[should] see all the creeps you have to put up with."

HAMILTON JORDAN

LINDA RONSTADT AND CALIFORNIA GOVERNOR JERRY BROWN/photo by Chuck Pulin

"I don't care if I'm called a Democrat
or a Republican as long as I'm in bed with people of the
same thinking."

SENATOR BARRY GOLDWATER

"I am working for the time when
unqualified blacks, browns, and women join the unqualified men
in running our government."

SISSY FARENTHOLD, TEXAS LEGISLATOR

"If they believe tomorrow that the American
populace loves people who walk around with their penises hanging out,
you can stand on Capitol Hill and watch every swinging dick walk by,
because they'll all have 'em out there."

DRAFT RESISTER DAVID HARRIS ON POLITICIANS, 1971

"Selling time to a political candidate
is like a criminal stealing a woman's wedding ring after he's raped her."

NICHOLAS JOHNSON, FORMER FCC COMMISSIONER

"You can fool some of the people
some of the time and jack the rest off."

ROBIN WILLIAMS CHARACTERIZING JIMMY CARTER

"A campaign is a sensual community of
the spirit. The smell of it, the taste of it . . . the feel of it. It's like a
good shot of cocaine right in the nose."

JACK VALENTI, PRESIDENT OF THE MOTION PICTURE ASSOCIATION AND
1964 CAMPAIGN AIDE TO LYNDON JOHNSON

"Kiss my ass."

SENATOR GEORGE McGOVERN TO A HECKLER IN THE WANING DAYS
OF HIS CAMPAIGN FOR THE PRESIDENCY

"I didn't bother to vote yesterday. I'm an anarchist,
anyway. I haven't really been interested in voting since they took
Norman Thomas off the ticket. I don't think it makes any
difference who has his duke in the till, really."

ACTOR ROBERT MITCHUM

"Now that I've won, I'm gonna
make Attila the Hun look like a faggot!"

FRANK RIZZO, ON BEING REELECTED MAYOR OF PHILADELPHIA

"My door is open, and I hope people
will come through the door rather than the window."

KENNETH GIBSON, MAYOR OF NEWARK, REACTING TO RIOTS THERE

"How many swan songs can a lame duck deliver?"

SECRETARY OF STATE HENRY KISSINGER
ON HIS MANY FAREWELL CEREMONIES

"It galls me, all those fools and assholes
calling it 'the government of the people,' while in actuality, most
politicians are just running their private games on people."

ROBERT REDFORD

"We were a large country, the opportunities
were great, the system for the white man was mostly unoppressive,
the lowest man could be president. And here, indeed, we
were right. The lowest man has been president."

LILLIAN HELLMAN

"The top leadership, the political fellas—
they ain't what they used to be. I think they got too worried about
what all them agitators, them civil liberties fellas, was sayin'."

CAPTAIN A.Y. ALLEE OF THE TEXAS RANGERS

"Greatness is lying in the streets
of Washington these days, and somebody may pick it up."

HENRY KISSINGER

"If there are souls in torment
because the secretary of defense travels in a limousine, I shall be quite
happy to abandon that limousine."

JAMES SCHLESINGER, SECRETARY OF DEFENSE

"Believe me, this was done over my dead body."

HENRY KISSINGER, DENYING A ROLE IN THE FIRING OF
SECRETARY OF DEFENSE JAMES SCHLESINGER

"Will the chancellor stop all unnecessary
spending for the underprivileged, including the 1000 pounds a week we
give to a parasite like Princess Margaret?"

DENNIS CANAVAN OF THE BRITISH LABOR PARTY

"If you were going to that kind of party, wouldn't you take a book?"

ROSALYN CARTER ON AMY'S PRACTICE OF
READING AT STATE DINNERS

"Now if it turns out
that we do the whole thing, sell everybody love, then we'll start
selling hate. The same machine will work."

VICTOR BARANCO, CO-FOUNDER OF THE INSTITUTE OF HUMAN
ABILITIES, A CHAIN OF PROFITABLE COMMUNES

"How many times
can they use those words—*justice*, *freedom*. It's like margarine, man.
You can package it and sell that, too. In America they have
a great talent for doing that."

KEITH RICHARDS

"Hype. What a marvelous, misused word.
If you hype something and it succeeds, you're a genius, it wasn't hype;
if you hype it and it fails, then it's just a hype."

NEIL BOGART, PRESIDENT OF CASABLANCA RECORDS

"Hey, a good-looking man with $10 million
who says the right things . . . I guarantee he could do it right using TV.
When I heard Ronald Reagan was running for governor of this
state, I thought it was a joke."

DIRECTOR HAL ASHBY ON TELEVISION'S POTENTIAL

"Nixon just isn't half the man Hitler was."

RICHARD DUDMAN, *ST. LOUIS POST-DISPATCH* CORRESPONDENT

"He told us he was going to take crime
out of the streets. He did. He took it to the damn White House."

REVEREND RALPH D. ABERNATHY ON RICHARD NIXON

❧

"The general secretary and I both
studied piano as young boys. Just think what would have happened
had we both become piano players! Music's loss
was détente's gain."

RICHARD NIXON, SPEAKING ABOUT HIMSELF AND LEONID BREZHNEV

❧

"The craziest thing he ever did
in his life was not to go to Vegas. He plays the piano, right? He could
get up there with his tapes and his piano and draw more than
Elvis. I'd pay to see him."

ALICE COOPER ON RICHARD NIXON

❧

"My father is going to fulfill
the mandate he was given to rule the country."

TRICIA NIXON COX AT A PRO-NIXON RALLY

❧

"People know that he cannot reign
as president. Everybody in the country is against him. I'll give him till
April at the latest."

MARTHA MITCHELL ON RICHARD NIXON IN 1973

❧

"Washington is like Paris during the Nazi occupation."

MAXINE CHESHIRE, *WASHINGTON POST* SOCIETY COLUMNIST,
ON NIXON'S FIRST YEAR

"Believe me, I have a high respect
for the bulldogged way in which our president has been able
to continue to administrate this government, in spite of the articulate
liberal press—whose only purpose is to sell toilet paper and
Toyotas—and in spite of the ambitious politicians."

JOHN WAYNE DURING THE NIXON ADMINISTRATION

"Everybody jumped on my back
and I had to deal with it alone. Only my wife and a few close friends
knew what happened. It was like open-heart surgery with
no Novocaine or anesthesia of any kind."

SAMMY DAVIS, JR., ON THE CRITICISM HE RECEIVED FOR HIS 1972
ENDORSEMENT OF NIXON

"A Nixon-Agnew administration will
abolish the credibility gap and reestablish the truth—the whole truth—
as its policy."

SPIRO AGNEW

"Mama suggested I do it to show Dad I love him."

E. HOWARD HUNT'S DAUGHTER, LISA HUNT, EXPLAINING WHY
SHE VOTED FOR NIXON

"I'd rather vote for a dead guy with class than two live bums."

BILL VEECK, FORMER BASEBALL COMMISSIONER, EXPLAINING WHY HE VOTED
FOR NORMAN THOMAS FOR PRESIDENT IN 1972

"Clearly, President Nixon wants me
to do this, just as he did it for President Eisenhower. It's the most
virile role I have."

SPIRO AGNEW ON HIS ROLE AS VICE-PRESIDENT

"If you've got 'em by the balls,
their hearts and minds will follow."

SIGN IN THE WHITE HOUSE OFFICE OF CHARLES COLSON,
AIDE TO PRESIDENT NIXON

"The charges against me are,
if you'll pardon the expression, damned lies. I am innocent of these
charges. If indicted, I will not resign."

SPIRO AGNEW, LATE SUMMER 1973

"As President Nixon said, presidents can
do almost anything, and President Nixon has done many things
nobody would have thought of doing."

GOLDA MEIR AT A STATE BANQUET FOR RICHARD NIXON IN JERUSALEM

"I'm still behind the man 100 percent—
but to tell you the truth, an impeachment hearing on television
would be so much more interesting than all those
summer reruns that we get nowadays."

GEORGE LEHN, RETIRED EXECUTIVE AT LEISURE WORLD
IN LAGUNA HILLS, CALIFORNIA

"He is our president, and I feel that if Richard Nixon is
impeached, there will be mass suicides, mass nervous breakdowns,
and total demoralization of the country."

MRS. HELEN BUFFINGTON, BRANCH VICE-CHAIRPERSON,
COMMITTEE TO REELECT THE PRESIDENT

"I fully believe that every detractor of President Nixon
will come before the bar of justice, either in this lifetime
or the next."

RABBI BARUCH KORFF

"I gave 'em a sword. And they
stuck it in, and they twisted it with relish. And I guess if I had been in
their position, I'd have done the same thing."

RICHARD NIXON ON WATERGATE

"Watergate is the president's Becket,
and like Henry II, he cannot escape the full brunt of responsibility
for his subordinates."

VICTOR GOLD, FORMER PRESS SECRETARY TO VICE PRESIDENT AGNEW

"Now it's like the French Revolution.
I feel like Mme. LaFarge knitting in the names as if the guillotine
was out in the square. We sit here waiting for more
heads to roll."

MAXINE CHESHIRE, *WASHINGTON POST* SOCIETY COLUMNIST,
ON WASHINGTON AFTER WATERGATE

"Watergate is not primarily a story of political
espionage, nor even of White House intrigue. It is a particularly
malodorous chapter in the annals of campaign financing. The
money paid to Watergate conspirators before the break-in . . .
and the money passed to them later . . . was money
from campaign gifts. It was not found
in a pea patch."

JOHN W. GARDNER, FORMER CHAIRMAN OF COMMON CAUSE

"That's fucked, but that's
politics, and politics are fucked, basically."

SAINT HUNT, E. HOWARD HUNT'S SON, ON THE WATERGATE BREAK-INS

"Obviously I would never do it again. I'm too old, I'm too decrepit."

E. HOWARD HUNT ON HIS ROLE IN WATERGATE

"We elected him president
and he has a right to use his judgment on what he should break into."

LOBBYIST FOR THE CITIZENS' CONGRESS FOR FAIRNESS
TO THE PRESIDENT

"I think the GOP and the rest of the nation
will realize that this was just seven men who made a mistake, and
others made a mistake by trying to cover it up."

JULIE NIXON EISENHOWER ON WATERGATE

"It's an easy name to spell. Only five letters."

CHARLES COLSON, TELLING WHY HIS NAME CAME UP SO OFTEN IN THE
WATERGATE TESTIMONY OF HIS FORMER COLLEAGUES

"Jesus came to me in a dream and told me Colson was a fraud."

JAYSON WECHTER, WHO HIT CHARLES COLSON WITH A PIE

"We felt they were doing things in the course of
the normal working day. They weren't sneaking around, or anything."

SYBIL KUCHARSKI, JURY FOREWOMAN OF THE MITCHELL-STANS TRIAL,
EXPLAINING THE VERDICT OF NOT GUILTY

"If you want to be a secretary
in Washington, you have to be able to erase 120 words a minute."

ART BUCHWALD, SPEAKING AT A COLLEGE COMMENCEMENT

"I don't know how many shoes
there are yet to fall. I feel like I've been dealing with a centipede
this last year."

SENATOR WILLIAM BROCK REACTING TO NEWS OF THE TAPE ERASURES

"The Lord is listening all the time.
The Lord has got his tape recorder going from the time you're born
until you die."

BILLY GRAHAM

"What's wrong with taping a conversation
when you happen to have a tape recorder with you? Most people in
America love playing with tape recorders."

MAO ZEDONG ON RICHARD NIXON

"Mr. Haldeman has every right
to be considered guilty until proven guilty."

RICHARD NIXON IN A SPEECH TO RESTORE CONFIDENCE IN THE PRESIDENCY

"We say . . . come the revolution,
be sure and save two bullets: one for Haldeman and one for Ehrlichman."

SECRET SERVICEMAN QUOTED IN *THE PALACE GUARD* BY DAN RATHER
AND GARY GATES

"If the president turns out to be guilty, I don't want to hear about it."

MELVIN LAIRD, WHITE HOUSE CHIEF OF STAFF IN 1979

"I don't want to be on the bookshelves with everybody else."

RON ZIEGLER, RICHARD NIXON'S WHITE HOUSE PRESS SECRETARY

"That would be like hearing from a call girl who gave you a dose."

FRANK DE MARCO, NIXON'S FORMER TAX ATTORNEY, WHEN ASKED
IF HE'D HEARD FROM THE EX-PRESIDENT LATELY

"I've made peace with myself
on the grounds—it's corny, but we've all sinned, right? There's more
rejoicing over the one lost sheep that is found."

JEB MAGRUDER ON HIS ROLE IN WATERGATE

"I'm feeling fine. Luckily this
doesn't affect the brain. Mentally, I'm okay."

RICHARD NIXON ON HIS PHLEBITIS

"He's coming along fine. He was
depressed, but he's on his way back. He's in better health than I've
seen him in a long time . . . Pray for him . . . and for me."

ROSE MARY WOODS, THE PRESIDENT'S SECRETARY

"I only wish to God I'd been on
the Watergate committee. I think the questioning would have been a
little bit stronger and more pertinent, very candidly."

HOWARD COSELL

"I'm surprised he said something nice
about me. Sometimes I wish I was a dog and Howard was a tree."

MUHAMMAD ALI ON HOWARD COSELL

"Why were we ever stupid enough to think
that this awful man would fade away like one of MacArthur's old
soldiers? He was always going to be dragged, kicking and
screaming, into oblivion."

REPRESENTATIVE JOHN ANDERSON ON RICHARD NIXON IN 1974

"This country needs good farmers, good businessmen, good plumbers."

RICHARD NIXON, IN HIS FAREWELL SPEECH TO HIS STAFF

"Peaceful Coup d'Etat in U.S.: Nixon Overthrown;
Victory for the U.S. Press, Congress after a 672 Day
Protracted Struggle"

HEADLINE IN SOUTH VIETNAMESE NEWSPAPER

"Richard Nixon impeached
himself. He gave us Gerald Ford as his revenge."

REPRESENTATIVE BELLA ABZUG

"I strongly support the feeding of children."

GERALD FORD ON THE SCHOOL LUNCH BILL

"I share your deep appreciation
about the increased irreverence for life."

GERALD FORD IN A SPEECH TO THE FORTY-FIRST EUCHARISTIC CONGRESS

"It's for historical purposes, I guess."

GERALD FORD, EXPLAINING WHY HE WAS TAPING A CONVERSATION
WITH HENRY KISSINGER

"Well, as far as I know personally,
there are no people presently employed in the White House who have
a relationship with the CIA of which I am personally unaware."

GERALD FORD

"To the great people
of the government of Israel. Excuse me—of Egypt."

PRESIDENT FORD PROPOSING A TOAST AT A DINNER IN HIS HONOR
GIVEN BY EGYPTIAN PRESIDENT ANWAR SADAT

"I'm a great fan of baseball.
I watch a lot of games on the radio, er, I mean television."

GERALD FORD

"The president looked at his
pool this morning. The president did not take a swim."

RON NESSEN BRIEFING THE WHITE HOUSE PRESS, DURING
THE FORD ADMINISTRATION

"I've never seen him relax more intensely."

WHITE HOUSE AIDE DESCRIBING PRESIDENT FORD ON HIS VACATION
IN VAIL, COLORADO

"All the American presidents
looked backward until Nixon. President Nixon looked forward.
President Ford is just looking."

A CHINESE OFFICIAL

"Sometimes I'm for it and sometimes I'm against it."

STEVEN FORD ON LEGALIZATION OF MARIJUANA

"My room is all right. But then
there's that feeling that you'll round the corner wearing just your
shorts—and run into a group of tourists."

JACK FORD ON LIFE IN THE WHITE HOUSE

"There is no way I want to get into politics,
and I can't think of anything worse than my father going through a
national campaign."

JOHN FORD

"I've had to prove that I can get jobs because I'm
a good photographer and not just because my name is Susan Ford."

THE PRESIDENT'S DAUGHTER ON EARNING $100,000 IN ONE YEAR

"I don't think you'll have to worry that this
mental midget, this hillbilly Hitler from Alabama, is anywhere near
becoming the nominee of the Democratic party."

JULIAN BOND ON ALABAMA GOVERNOR GEORGE WALLACE

"I support Wallace about as much
as your average American supported Hitler."

LEON WILKESON OF LYNYRD SKYNYRD, AFTER GEORGE WALLACE PROCLAIMED
THE GROUP HONORARY LIEUTENANT COLONELS IN ALABAMA'S STATE
MILITIA FOR THEIR ACHIEVEMENTS IN MUSIC

"It's high time the red necks came back
to Washington. There are a hell of a lot more red necks out there than
people who eat crêpes suzette."

MICKEY GRIFFIN, CAMPAIGN ORGANIZER FOR GEORGE WALLACE

"I would have a fairly steady stream of visitors,
just average Americans . . . to come in and spend a night with us
at the White House and eat supper with us."

JIMMY CARTER

"He says his lust is in his heart. I hope it's a little lower."

SHIRLEY MacLAINE ON JIMMY CARTER

"How many of you have been
on your knees in the past twenty-four hours? I have."

JIMMY CARTER

"For a working man or woman
to vote Republican this year is the same as a chicken voting for
Colonel Sanders."

WALTER MONDALE

"There are two Jimmy Carters: one running
for president and one governor of Georgia, and let me tell you one
thing. If Richard Nixon had gotten his training from
Jimmy Carter, he never would have gotten caught."

LESTER MADDOX, FORMER GOVERNOR OF GEORGIA

"It was very nice of Ford. He has picked
a known hitman, a hit artist, a man who is recognized everywhere
as a hired gun."

BARRY JAGOTA, JIMMY CARTER'S PRESS AIDE, ON PRESIDENT FORD'S
RUNNING MATE, SENATOR ROBERT F. DOLE

"If Ford can get away with this list of issues . . .
and be elected on it, then I'm going to call the dictator of Uganda,
Mr. Amin, and tell him to start giving speeches
on airport safety."

WALTER MONDALE, 1976 DEMOCRATIC VICE-PRESIDENTIAL CANDIDATE

"I have never seen a man so much at peace
with himself. It would take me seven doubles to find such peace,
and then I wouldn't understand it."

STUART SPENCER, FORD'S DEPUTY CAMPAIGN MANAGER, DESCRIBING FORD
ON THE MORNING OF HIS DEFEAT

"It sure is nice to have
a president who don't speak with an accent."

LORETTA LYNN ON JIMMY CARTER'S ELECTION IN 1976

"The loudest sound heard in Atlanta was
the quiet clicks of thousands of suitcase locks closing
for the great exodus."

JULIAN BOND AFTER JIMMY CARTER WON THE PRESIDENCY

"If, after the inauguration,
you find a Cy Vance as secretary of state
and Zbigniew Brzezinski as head of national security,
then I would say we've failed. And I'd quit. But that's not going to
happen. You're going to see new faces, new ideas. The
government is going to be run by people
you never heard of."

HAMILTON JORDAN IN NOVEMBER 1976

"He didn't even invite me to sing
at the inauguration. He had Charlie Daniels to sing. I never heard him
quote any Charlie Daniels song."

BOB DYLAN, QUOTED BY JIMMY CARTER IN HIS AUTOBIOGRAPHY
AND IN HIS ACCEPTANCE SPEECH AT THE DEMOCRATIC CONVENTION

"When you go to the White House, the place looks
physically dirty; people running around in jeans doesn't look right . . .
It just seems the government doesn't know what they are doing."

SENATOR EDWARD W. BROOKE, AT THE OUTSET OF THE
CARTER ADMINISTRATION

"It's a period of transition that has its ups and downs.
There's the initial temptation to pick up the telephone and tell
somebody what to do. It takes a while to realize there's
no one at the other end of the telephone."

HENRY KISSINGER, IN 1977

"I told the president I would handle the problem
[media criticism for placing his personal chef on the public payroll]
. . . . I'm rewriting the job description."

JOSEPH CALIFANO, SECRETARY OF THE DEPARTMENT OF HEALTH,
EDUCATION AND WELFARE IN 1977

"Human rights is suddenly chic. For years
we were preachers, cockeyed idealists or busybodies, and now
we are respectable."

ROBERTA COHEN, EXECUTIVE DIRECTOR OF THE INTERNATIONAL
LEAGUE FOR HUMAN RIGHTS

"Jimmy and I are so close,
we used to sleep in the same bed."

ERWIN DAVID RABHAN, GEORGIA BUSINESSMAN

"You can come anytime, for whatever.
If the president did something I thought was great and I was caught up
in it, I'd have an orgasm. But he ain't did that to me yet."

SARAH DASH, OF LABELLE

"Jimmy Carter is a Christian, but
he's a McGovern-type Christian—proabortion, prohomosexuality, and
prolegalizing marijuana."

PAT BOONE

"When the president's son says drug use is okay, man, that is a sickness."

LOS ANGELES POLICE CHIEF ED DAVIS

"I think that when they talk about the Indians smoking
the peace pipe, I believe when the Indians came over the hill that they
was high. I believe that pipe the Indians were smoking was full
of Acapulco Gold mixed with a little hashish."

LITTLE RICHARD

"If the cannabis epidemic continues to spread
at the rate of the post-Berkeley period, we may find ourselves
saddled with a large population of semizombies—of young people
acutely afflicted by the amotivational syndrome."

SENATOR JAMES EASTLAND

"They're very definitely going to legalize it
pretty soon, because all of the law students are users."

LENNY BRUCE ON MARIJUANA

"That obviously would be an incredible yield.
Somebody must have smoked some awfully good dope to come up
with that conclusion."

CALIFORNIA ASSEMBLYMAN WILLIE BROWN, REPLYING TO STATE ATTORNEY
GENERAL EVELLE YOUNGER'S ASSERTION THAT SIX MARIJUANA PLANTS
COULD PRODUCE 18,000 CIGARETTES

"I just bet the United States government could
kick itself in the ass for planting 10,000 acres of marijuana here. I just
bet they could."

JACK OSBORN, SHERIFF OF JASPER COUNTY, INDIANA

"I tried marijuana one time, but it didn't do
anything for me, 'cept give me a headache. Sheeeet, I played a gig
with the Doors once, and those boys smoked so much of that
stuff you could get a headache just walkin' into
their dressin' room."

GLEN CAMPBELL

"If you were on a plane
and the pilot was drunk, you could tell, but if he was on
marijuana, you couldn't."

RONALD REAGAN, ARGUING AGAINST POT

"They again showed their determined effort
to destroy America by claiming that kids have a constitutional right
to use dope while they are attending school."

ED DAVIS, LOS ANGELES POLICE CHIEF, REACTING TO AN ACLU SUIT TO BAR
FUNDS FOR PAYMENT OF UNDERCOVER AGENTS IN PUBLIC SCHOOLS

"So who cares? What responsibility does our government
have for dope smokers who might be poisoned with paraquat?"

U.S. OFFICIALS, QUOTED BY SENATOR CHARLES PERCY

"Since pot is against the law, the government
has no legal responsibility to protect people who smoke it."

DR. PETER BOURNE, JIMMY CARTER'S ADVISOR ON DRUG POLICY,
COMMENTING ON THE DANGERS OF PARAQUAT

"It's been reported that hashish caused the death
of Baudelaire, but this report overlooks the fact that Baudelaire was
an alcoholic with terminal syphilis."

DR. PETER LOMAX OF UCLA

"I do not believe that the Bible teaches teetotalism.
Jesus drank wine. Jesus turned water into wine at a wedding feast.
That wasn't grape juice as some of them try to claim."

BILLY GRAHAM

"I come from a family 1000 percent alcoholic. I wish
to Christ a couple of them would have used a little cocaine or
something to slow it up a little bit. Whiskey wrecked my family. But
frankly, I prefer whiskey to LSD."

JIMMY BRESLIN

"Partly to forget everything—which is
what booze is about—and partly because I couldn't find anything
decent to smoke in America."

JOE COCKER ON WHY HE DRINKS

"You can OD on creamed spinach
but not on the SX-70. Since I quit booze, I had to spend my money on
some addiction. Anything you don't swallow is all right."

GRACE SLICK ON HER POLAROID CAMERA

GRACE SLICK OF THE JEFFERSON STARSHIP/photo by David Gahr

"I tried it once and it gave me diarrhea."

LILLIAN CARTER ON BILLY BEER, NAMED AFTER HER SON

"It's easy to get along with everyone when
you're shitfaced smashed all the time. The fun thing about being sober
is meeting all the friends I've had for years—especially the ones
I've never met."

ALICE COOPER

"It's easier to get people off of heroin than coffee."

DR. RICHARD T. RAPPOLT, WHO TREATS
HEROIN ADDICTS

"I've been living on 'Sister Morphine' for
ten years, which is really bizarre—don't tell me drugs don't pay!"

MARIANNE FAITHFULL ON SONGWRITING ROYALTIES

"Loosen up wasn't the word—try fucked up;
instead of gettin' drunk every night before the gig, we'd just smoke
a little grass, drop half a tab and cut loose. It really helps you
get into the music."

STUD MITCHELL OF THE WILD THING

"People who say they take drugs for a mystical
or religious experience are full of shit, man. It gets you high. That's
its only redeeming feature."

JAMES TAYLOR

"Your mind is a great thing—
especially when you're hallucinating."

PAUL McCARTNEY TALKING ABOUT IMAGES EMPLOYED IN "SGT. PEPPER"

"Don't use speed! It'll mess up your liver,
your heart and kidneys, and screw your mind up and in general will
make you just like your parents."

FRANK ZAPPA

"As far as the coaches were concerned,
a guy could shoot kerosene if it didn't hurt his game. The increased use of
grass and other psychedelics among football players
is one of the things that is going to change
the game radically."

CHIP OLIVER OF THE OAKLAND RAIDERS

"Chip wasn't a dropout, he was a cop-out.
He says that he once kicked a seventy-five-yard field goal in practice while
he was high on mescaline. My answer to that is that I once punted
eighty-six yards at the University of Kentucky. At the time
I was high on Polish sausage."

OAKLAND RAIDER QUARTERBACK GEORGE BLANDA ON TEAMMATE CHIP OLIVER'S
ADMITTED DRUG USE

"Must you lay down your Fate to the Lord High Alchemy
in the hands of the Chalk and the Drug? Magic circles he will spin and
dirges he will sing through the transparency
of a Queen Ant's Wing."

DONOVAN'S PLEA TO YOUTH TO STOP USING DRUGS

ELDRIDGE CLEAVER/photo by UPI

"Being programmed by dope talk
or any of that stuff is like somebody trying to tell you what it's like
to fuck if you've never fucked anybody."

JERRY GARCIA

"The world is having a nervous breakdown.
Valium is the only glue that holds it together."

ARTHUR JANOV, PRIMAL THERAPIST

"I got up several hills thanks to some good benzedrine."

CIA DIRECTOR WILLIAM COLBY CITING HIS WORLD WAR II EXPERIENCES
TO DEFEND THE AGENCY'S USE OF DRUGS IN OPERATIONS

"It was never really effective,
but it helped psychologically because the people who used it didn't
know it wasn't effective."

DR. C. SCOTT JOHNSON OF THE SAN DIEGO NAVAL UNDERSEA CENTER
DESCRIBING CHEMICAL SHARK REPELLANT ISSUED BY THE
MILITARY SINCE WORLD WAR II

"I smoked fifty joints
in the sixties and snorted two lines of coke once in Detroit. It wasn't half
as nice as a good lady . . . or a good meal, for that matter."

TED NUGENT

"I think that the use of LSD, as it is manifested in the
high priest of LSD, Dr. Timothy Leary, brings 1984 with all of its
horrible ramifications so much closer. That's not the future
that we are fighting and dying for."

ELDRIDGE CLEAVER

"I missed that generation
by about five years—that and the sexual revolution."

JODY POWELL, 34, ON DRUG USE AMONG YOUTH

"I panicked at the thought
of being away from home and not being able to get cocaine."

FILM DIRECTOR STAN DRAGOTI AFTER PLEADING GUILTY TO BRINGING COCAINE
INTO WEST GERMANY

"The soundest reports on the drug culture
I found in the *Wall Street Journal*. These people are much more in tune
with the individual American than politicians are. You have
a stronger vote as a buyer than as a voter; you can
put them out of business."

STEWART BRAND OF *THE WHOLE EARTH CATALOG*

"I mean, first of all it's anticocaine.
I don't even like the stuff. And second, what's champagne going for
these days? Two bucks a bottle?"

TOM PETTY RESPONDING TO RECORD-COMPANY AND
RADIO-STATION PRESSURE TO CHANGE THE WORD
COCAINE TO *CHAMPAGNE* IN ONE OF HIS SONGS

"I need euphoria now and then myself.
And I haven't gotten nearly enough of it in my life."

REPRESENTATIVE CLARENCE LONG ON THE INTERNATIONAL
TRAFFICKING OF COCAINE

"If this transcript gets out,
you'll have even less euphoria."

REPRESENTATIVE BILL YOUNG REPLYING TO CLARENCE LONG

"To get high is to forget yourself.
And to forget yourself is to see everything else. And to see everything else
is to become an understanding molecule in evolution,
a conscious tool of the universe."

JERRY GARCIA

"Why does everyone cite Gregg Allman?
Linda Ronstadt had her nose cauterized and Jerry Brown dated her."

PHIL WALDEN, CAPRICORN RECORDS PRESIDENT, AFTER HE WAS ASKED WHY
PRESIDENT CARTER WOULD WANT TO ASSOCIATE WITH PERFORMERS
KNOWN FOR THEIR DRUG USE

"If you're rich, you can go to Switzerland
and have your blood changed. You know, there are a million ways how
the rich can get off drugs. But this is the ground root level, the
street-addict level. They only have a tiny percentage
of success."

MARIANNE FAITHFULL ON TREATING HEROIN ADDICTION

"Do the Stones use drugs? No, never."

MICK JAGGER

"If you get a member
of the Rolling Stones off heroin, you've done some good."

PAUL KENNEDY, CANADIAN CROWN PROSECUTOR, COMMENTING ON
KEITH RICHARDS' SUSPENDED SENTENCE AFTER HE WAS
CONVICTED FOR POSSESSION OF HEROIN IN 1978

"Maybe I'll get a song out of it."

KEITH RICHARDS' REACTION TO A 1977 CONVICTION FOR POSSESSION OF COCAINE

SONNY BONO AND CHER BONO ALLMAN/photo by Movie Star News

"There is no way we can work with Gregg
again ever. I mean, when you're sitting in court and a man who's
worked with you personally for two years and saved your life twice is
sitting there with his life on the line, and you walk into court and tap
on the mike and say, 'Testing, one, two, three,' which is a fact, it's
what Gregg did, 'Testing, one, two, three,' and Scooter's
sitting there with his fucking life on the line."

GUITARIST DICKEY BETTS, ANGERED AT GREGG ALLMAN'S BEHAVIOR
IN THE SCOOTER HERRING DRUG-BUST TRIAL

"I was scared to death to go in there
and have them ask me these things . . . It was either that or go to jail."

GREGG ALLMAN AFTER BEING GRANTED IMMUNITY FOR HIS TESTIMONY
AGAINST SCOOTER HERRING

"It was a terrible thing to do to
the people. I'm sure Republicans were probably behind that."

GREGG ALLMAN CRITICIZING A MAGAZINE COVER OF ALLMAN HOLDING A SPOON
OF COKE NEXT TO PHIL WALDEN AND JIMMY CARTER

"Our whole world was shot to ratshit . . . I ought to write a soap opera."

CHER BONO ALLMAN COMMENTING ON THE SCOOTER HERRING DRUG BUST

"I'm tired of being an actor in a soap opera."

GREGG ALLMAN ON PUBLICITY DURING THE SCOOTER HERRING DRUG BUST

"The TV audience
is a drug generation. It has already been stoned for ten years."

MARSHALL McLUHAN

"TV has eaten up everything else,
and Warhol films are all that are left. *Pork* could become the next
I Love Lucy."

DAVID BOWIE

"The pressure to give them less
is so great in television because the traffic will bear almost anything."

LORNE MICHAELS, PRODUCER OF *SATURDAY NIGHT LIVE*

"All TV I personally rate
right up there with foul air, shit in the seas, too many babies. The
spontaneity, the originality of a whole people is being
sucked out by that tube."

PETER FALK

"Mao Zedong didn't have to deal
with people who were watching seven hours of television every day."

ELAINE BROWN, BLACK PANTHER LEADER

"I like to talk on TV
about those things that aren't worth writing about."

TRUMAN CAPOTE

"The ultimate game show
will be the one where somebody gets killed at the end."

CHUCK BARRIS, GAME SHOW PRODUCER

"I would not rule out a bionic dog having his own show one day."

TV PRODUCER LEE SIEGEL

"When the Swiss Kriss Company
give me a radio show, my slogan will be, 'Everybody, this is Satchmo
speaking for Swiss Kriss. Are you Loosning?' "

LOUIS ARMSTRONG, ADVOCATING THE LAXATIVE

"I believed the show should look
as if the network had closed down and these guys snuck into the studio—
that it always be perceived as an underdog."

LORNE MICHAELS, PRODUCER OF *SATURDAY NIGHT LIVE*

"I've got to do this film because I don't want
to be remembered for doing a medley of my Clearasil commercials."

DICK CLARK ON *THE YEARS OF ROCK*

"When you look at ideas for hundreds of programs,
and they all happen to feature women with big bosoms, you know
there's a trend."

LYNN ROTH, DIRECTOR OF TV COMEDY DEVELOPMENT,
20TH CENTURY-FOX

"I don't want Anita Bryant to find out about this."

QUARTERBACK ROGER STAUBACH ON WEARING MAKEUP FOR A COMMERCIAL

"These shows bring out the worst
in human beings—I'm hypocritical and greedy enough myself to want to
make money out of it. Somebody recently called me
the king of slob culture."

CHUCK BARRIS, TV GAME SHOW PRODUCER

"The only thing that could
fuck it up now is what fucks up everything—success."

LORNE MICHAELS, PRODUCER OF *SATURDAY NIGHT LIVE*

"I look back on those as not the prime,
but the fucking good old days. We're all trying to get back to a simpler,
less aggravating way of life. I don't think we'll accomplish it."

DICK CLARK, LOOKING BACK AT *AMERICAN BANDSTAND*

"I got awfully tired of shouting 'Yay,' and sometimes
it seems we did nothing but jump up and down and shout 'Yay'—
and working with those godawful monkeys, and getting bored stiff
with most of the guest entertainers."

DENNIS DAY ON BEING A MOUSKETEER

"Like, I can't be on none of
those television shows, 'cause I'd have to tell Johnny Carson, 'You're
a sad motherfucker.' That's the only way I could put it."

MILES DAVIS

MILES DAVIS/photo by David Gahr

"The Fifties were terrible. I hate to see the Fifties
romanticized like they are in *Grease* or on *Happy Days*. If you had any
kind of sensitivity in the Fifties, someone was bound
to step on your head."

MUSICIAN BOB WELCH

"If Nixon had hired me, he'd still be president."

BOB JONES, VETERAN FILM EDITOR

"The blaxploitation films are
a phenomenon of self-hate. Look at the image of Superfly. Going to see
yourself as a drug dealer when you're oppressed is sick. Not only are the
blacks identifying with him, they're paying for the identification.
It's sort of like a Jew paying to get into Auschwitz."

TONY BROWN, DEAN OF HOWARD UNIVERSITY'S SCHOOL OF COMMUNICATION

"All we're saying in the film is what Terry Southern said
in his book: people will swim through shit if you put a few bob in it."

PETER SELLERS ON *THE MAGIC CHRISTIAN*

"A cardinal rule: always get yourself killed off
in a picture that looks like it's gonna be a success, sweetheart."

LEE MARVIN DISCUSSING MARLON BRANDO'S SUCCESS IN *THE GODFATHER*

"I don't think it's an
outrageously commercial film. It's just four walls and some people."

DUSTIN HOFFMAN ON HIS WORK IN *KRAMER VS. KRAMER*

"I've made so many movies playing a hooker
that they don't pay me in the regular way anymore. They leave it
on the dresser."

SHIRLEY MacLAINE

"I'd rather see *Bambi.*"

LORETTA LYNN ON THE FILM *NASHVILLE*

"If I can play God, I can certainly sing a Beatles song."

GEORGE BURNS ON HIS ROLE IN *SGT. PEPPER*

"You know the authority on all this
is Skinner, and his latest works state the premise that human freedom
and dignity have become inconsistent with the survival of our civilization.
It's a very startling and sinister and not totally refutable contention,
and *Clockwork Orange* is very concerned with this sort of idea."

STANLEY KUBRICK DISCUSSING HIS FILM

"The reason I thought up this movie
was to be in the dressing room to hear the conversation between Sly Stone
and Tiny Tim."

PAUL SIMON ON HIS ROCK & ROLL MOVIE *ONE TRICK PONY*

"Actors scare people. Everyone has this
schizoid attitude toward actors. They'll either elect them governor of
California or they won't let them into the tavern."

RICHARD DREYFUSS

"Film people are so fucking arrogant. I hate them.
I saw Sam Peckinpah. We went to the set of one of his films, and oh
dear, oh dear, I would have liked to have smashed him
right in the fucking mouth."

ELTON JOHN

"If I had to be everything I played I'd have a pretty fucked-up life."

JILL CLAYBURGH ON SEPARATING ART AND EXPERIENCE

"The governors of the music branch of the Academy are assholes."

ROBERT STIGWOOD, RSO RECORDS EXECUTIVE CHAIRMAN, AFTER
SATURDAY NIGHT FEVER WAS DENIED OSCAR NOMINATIONS

"I fall in love with all the actors in my films.
They are the prolongations of my penis. Yes, my penis. Like Pinocchio's
nose, my penis grows!"

DIRECTOR BERNARDO BERTOLUCCI

"Don't you know what they're doing
is fucking posters of Redford in the alleys of Rome? You don't have to
worry about acting. All you need is to get a poster they can fuck
in the alleys of Rome."

RAQUEL WELCH

"I really had to act, 'cause I didn't have any lines."

MARILYN CHAMBERS ON HER ROLE IN THE PORN FILM *BEHIND THE GREEN DOOR*

"I've got it. I'll show him hangin' himself by his own dick."

CARTOONIST BILL MAULDIN ON HARRY REEMS, WHO WAS ARRESTED
FOR CO-STARRING IN *DEEP THROAT*

"I think that in pornography lies the hope of America.
It can serve as the great unifier. Pornography is the great leveler of shame.
Louis XIV said, *'Apres moi, le deluge.'* I say, 'After
pornography, nothing.' "

ALAN BELL, PORNOGRAPHER

"I personally prefer to look at a nude woman
in a photo than a nude guy. I think it's no put-down to pose that way.
I think the women who resent it are those who are afraid
to admit they couldn't get into *Playboy*."

BARBI BENTON

"Rock music is the most brutal, ugly, vicious form
of expression . . . sly, lewd—in plain fact, dirty . . . [a] rancid-smelling
aphrodisiac . . . martial music of every delinquent on the face of the earth."

FRANK SINATRA, IN THE *NEW YORK POST*, OCTOBER 29, 1957

"I'd say Ray Charles was much better received
than President Carter, who came in two weeks before. But then, he's so
much more musical than the president."

JULIAN BOND, GEORGIA STATE SENATOR, AFTER THE SINGER VISITED THE STATE'S
LEGISLATURE, WHICH HAD JUST ADOPTED HIS ARRANGEMENT OF "GEORGIA
ON MY MIND" AS THE OFFICIAL STATE SONG

"I really like rock music, and Bob Dylan and I
get along really well. I care for these people, I respect them. They are
performers who lead strange lives as viewed from the eyes
of a peanut farmer."

JIMMY CARTER

"We do have our own ideas . . .
With a bit of cooperation on your part we might persuade
Paper Lace . . . to come to Chicago and jump in the Chicago River,
placing their heads under the water three times and surfacing twice.
"The lyrics are the greatest assemblage of garbage ever to be
published. Our interest is zero minus. Thank you for
contacting us. Pray tell us, are you nuts?"

MAYOR RICHARD DALEY'S OFFICE, RESPONDING TO A REQUEST FOR SUGGESTIONS
ON HOW TO PROMOTE A CONCERT BY PAPER LACE IN CHICAGO

"The main thing is to get the kids. You know, this is
the Catholic trick—they nail you when you're young and brainwash you,
and then they've got you for the rest of your life."

GEORGE HARRISON ON YOUTH "TURNING ON" WITH MUSIC

"Four hundred girls in the Detroit area, interviewed as to why
they had illegitimate babies, said it was not just the words but the beat.
The fertility rites of the jungle are the same beats recorded into
modern rock to stir them up."

DR. JACK VAN IMPE, CRUSADER AGAINST ROCK MUSIC

"If I really knew how to write, I could write something
that someone would read and it would kill them. The same way with
music, or any effect you want—[it] could be produced if you were
precise enough in your knowledge or technique."

WILLIAM BURROUGHS

The energy crisis has done for big car sales what pantyhose did for finger fucking.

You can fool some of the people some of the time and just the rest off.

— Robin Williams

Why the hell should I get a wife when the woman next door has one?

"I generally play rock music [over speakers] when
I perform open-heart operations. It's a long-proven observation that the
rhythm of music played in the background will set a tempo for work.
And it also helps ease the tension among the operating team."

DR. GERALD LeMOLE OF PHILADELPHIA, QUOTED IN THE *CHICAGO DAILY NEWS*

"When a record is recorded in front of 3 million people
by anyone who has his kind of influence and prestige, it doesn't hurt to
have that kind of representation in your company."

RON ALEXENBURG, PRESIDENT OF INFINITY RECORDS, ON WHY HE RELEASED
A RECORD BY POPE JOHN PAUL II

"Kids are more influenced by us than Jesus."

JOHN LENNON

"I rued the day that the Beatles were unfortunately born
into this world. They are, in my mind, responsible for most of the
degeneration that has happened, not only musically, but in the sense of
youth orientation politically, too. They are the people who first made it
publicly acceptable to spit in the eye of authority."

FRANK SINATRA, JR.

"The Beatles and their mimics use
Pavlovian techniques to provoke neurosis in their listeners."

REPRESENTATIVE JAMES UTT

"I think music is the main interest
of the younger people. It doesn't really matter about the older people
now, because they're finished anyway."

GEORGE HARRISON

"You cannot reheat a soufflé."

PAUL McCARTNEY ON ATTEMPTS TO REUNITE THE BEATLES

"God, it's like asking Liz Taylor
when she's going to get together with Eddie Fisher again."

LINDA McCARTNEY, TIRED OF QUERIES ABOUT A BEATLES REUNION

"Music always is a commentary on society,
and certainly the atrocities onstage are quite mild compared to those
conducted in our behalf by our government. You can't write a chord
ugly enough to say what you want to say sometimes, so you have to
rely on a giraffe filled with whipped cream."

FRANK ZAPPA ON HIS ACT

"It's like suddenly everybody getting hung up on a bum
trip. Mother has just fallen down the stairs, Dad's lost all his money
at the dog track, the baby's got TB. In comes the kid, man, with
his transistor radio, grooving to Chuck Berry. He doesn't give a shit about
Mom falling down the stairs. He's with rock & roll. That's what rock & roll
says to life. It says, you know, I'm hip, I'm happy, forget your
troubles and just enjoy! And, of course, this is the
biggest thing it has to offer."

PETE TOWNSHEND

"It's like taking a shit.
I guess a lotta people who can't write songs,
instead of writing songs, they'll get drunk and kick out a window."

WILLIE NELSON ON THE THERAPEUTIC VALUE OF SONGWRITING

ANDY WARHOL AND WILLIE NELSON/photo by Richard E. Aaron

"It's only rock & roll, disposable crap."

TOM PETTY ON HIS MUSIC

"John Sebastian sings a song about kids
and everyone applauds. A guy spells out fuck and everyone shouts.
There's no discrimination or real art involved in it at all."

WOODY ALLEN ON THE WOODSTOCK NATION

"I got into music 'cause I couldn't get into athletics."

JACKSON BROWNE

"You don't choose to play music; it chooses to play you."

MEL LYMAN, IN *FESTIVAL*, A FILM ABOUT THE NEWPORT FOLK FESTIVAL

"Music is a metaphor for everything."

WRITER-ILLUSTRATOR MAURICE SENDAK

"Music is medicine that's pleasant to take."

ODETTA

"I wouldn't want to have an orgasm
twenty-four hours a day. That wouldn't be any fun, would it?"

HERB ALPERT ON THE RARITY OF ACHIEVING A TRANSCENDENTAL
MOMENT IN MUSIC

"Yesterday's experiment is tomorrow's cliché."

MUSICIAN BOB WELCH ON MUSIC

"Everybody loves music. We could go to countries
where people are gruntin' to each other, and the music would get through."

VERDINE WHITE, OF EARTH, WIND, AND FIRE

"You won't make much money,
but you'll get more pussy than Frank Sinatry."

RONNIE HAWKINS ASKING ROBBIE ROBERTSON TO JOIN HIS BAND

"I've always been skeptical of the
rock & roll machismo thing. . . . Today it's just cooler to be a bad,
unhappy musician than a laid-out, cool bank teller. In five
years it's going to be hipper to be a bank clerk."

JAZZ PIANIST BEN SIDRAN

"I believe rock can do anything—
it's the ultimate vehicle for everything. It's the ultimate vehicle
for saying anything, for putting down anything, for
building up anything, for killing and creating. It's the
absolute ultimate vehicle for self-destruction, which is the most incredible
thing, because there's nothing as effective as that—not in terms of art,
anyway, or what we call art. You just can't be as effectively self-
destructive if you're a writer, for example, or a painter; you
just can't make sure that you're never going to fucking
raise your head again. Whereas if you're
a rock star you really can."

PETE TOWNSHEND

"We call it fag rock in the business. Of all the
degeneration that's happened since rock music came in, that's the worst."

FRANK SINATRA, JR., ON PUNK ROCK

🌿

"I think musicians are a strange type
of clergy among us. They're the closest we have to saints these days."

D.A. PENNEBAKER, WHO FILMED *MONTEREY POP*

🌿

If we played it straight like Gandhi
and Martin Luther King, we wouldn't be here. The thing is
people don't like saints. And we're not going to be saints, crucified or
otherwise. So, we keep throwing in a bit of shit."

JOHN LENNON, AFTER HE RETURNED HIS ORDER
OF THE BRITISH EMPIRE MEDAL

🌿

"I can't picture Jesus Christ doin' a whole lotta shakin'."

JERRY LEE LEWIS, WHO BELIEVES HE WILL GO TO HELL FOR PLAYING ROCK & ROLL

🌿

"I don't mind no religion. But we don't
nail our dicks to the cross, either. As for my pants, well, hey, that
Nur'yev feller wears them same kinda britches. I like to dance, too."

JIM DANDY, OF BLACK OAK ARKANSAS, BRANDED AS SINFUL AND LEWD
BY SOUTHERN PREACHERS FOR HIS PHALLIC BOOGIE

🌿

"God's doin' the jerk, and it's the jerk's fault for lettin' him do it."

CAPTAIN BEEFHEART

JONI MITCHELL/photo by James Shive

"So much of music is politics. It's going
for the big vote. It amounts to a lot of baby kissing."

JONI MITCHELL

"Pop music is just long hours, hard work, and a lot of drugs."

MAMA CASS ELLIOT

"The idea is to keep it as
simplistic, as innocent, as unassuming, and as stupid as possible."

DAVID LEE ROTH, VAN HALEN'S LEAD SINGER

"I think it should be tarted up, made into
a prostitute, a parody of itself. It should be the clown, the Pierrot
medium. The music is the mask the message wears—music is the
Pierrot and I, the performer, am the message."

DAVID BOWIE ON THE PURPOSE OF MUSIC

"We ain't never played no fruit rock,
no punk rock. We never wore dresses onstage, put no paint
on our faces, blew up no bombs onstage. We didn't suck off snakes
onstage; we didn't wear tight pants and big rings. We didn't pee-uke
onstage or throw TVs out the windas."

LEVON HELM OF THE BAND

"People expect if you're a star you should
look like one. I don't want to let them down—they deserve
flash and flair. . . . You don't play baseball with a tennis racket."

JOHNNY GUITAR WATSON ON HIS FLASHY IMAGE

"President Kennedy just saw the shit right quick.
He said, 'He ain't no gangster; he's just a junkie playing music.' "

JAZZ ARTIST HAMPTON HAWES ON HIS PRESIDENTIAL PARDON

"Hula hoops were once the most popular thing.
The public was masturbating with hula hoops; now it's guitars.
Guitars are easy, they're cheap; everybody plays them."

MIKE BLOOMFIELD, BLUES GUITARIST

"I don't make guitar-type comments.
I don't talk guitar talk, I just throw the thing around."

PETE TOWNSHEND, ASKED WHO WAS HIS FAVORITE GUITARIST

"It's almost like traveling to different cities with art.
You know, like bringing King Tut to America. Only my guitars are better
looking than King Tut."

CHEAP TRICK'S RICK NIELSEN, ON TRAVELING WITH HIS GUITAR COLLECTION

"It's been through three wives.
To me a guitar is kind of like a woman. You don't know why you like
'em, but you do."

WAYLON JENNINGS ON HIS TELECASTER

"Man, any four cats on earth
who can play three chords together can make an album. You need $500?
Just learn three chords and you've got it."

DUANE ALLMAN

"The first musical instrument I played was myself."

MARTY BALIN

"I don't play no music except what's
inside me. I'm no psychedelic man—I'm a Frenchman!"

CLIFTON CHENIER

"I think I can put together a better rock band than Jimi Hendrix."

MILES DAVIS, 1970

"I want a concept of
'Otis Redding meets *Star Wars*'—Really modern, but hard, cold funk."

ETTA JAMES ON HER STYLE

"My band is a dictatorship and Edgar's is a democracy."

JOHNNY WINTER, 1975

"I wanted to perform, I wanted
to write songs, and I wanted to get lots of chicks."

JAMES TAYLOR, WHEN ASKED WHY HE GOT INTO MUSIC

"I don't know fuck about the UN. I'd rather sing
about rock & roll and chicks. I think I'm much more in touch with that."

TOM PETTY

"I like to think of us as Clearasil on the face of the nation.
Jim Morrison would have said that if he was smart, but he's dead."

LOU REED ON HIS BAND'S TOUR

"So she couldn't sue me."

RAMONA MOORE, SURGICALLY ALTERED TO RESEMBLE JANIS JOPLIN,
ON WHY SHE PICKED A DEAD ARTIST TO EMULATE

"All the white groups have got a lot of hair
and funny clothes—they got to have that shit on to get it across. . . .
These bourgeois spades are trying to sing white, and the whites are trying
to sing colored. It's embarrassing. It's like me wearing a dress."

MILES DAVIS

"One of the popular slang terms is 'kinky,' meaning
personal perversion, and this mood seems to prevail in a lot of groups.
I've seen bands doing queer bits in their underwear to get attention."

GUITARIST STEVE MILLER ON THE BRITISH ROCK SCENE

"We were all reading about the Hopis,
and in the Hopi mythology the eagle is the most sacred animal
with the most spiritual meaning—the best that a man can be. Glenn [Frey]
likes the name for a different reason. Glenn likes the name because it
sounds like a teenage gang."

BERNIE LEADON, FORMER BASS PLAYER FOR THE EAGLES

"I can sing better
after shooting smack in both arms than after eating too much."

LINDA RONSTADT ON OVEREATING

GENE SIMMONS OF KISS/photo by Movie Star News

"I still have some tapes of the first time
I sang onstage at some club in Daytona. It is just purely awful noise.
I sound like a cross between Hank Williams with the croup and
James Brown with no lips."

GREGG ALLMAN ON HIS FIRST SINGING EFFORTS

"I was called Rubber Lips.
Then the Stones appeared and it was hip
to have big lips. I was able to talk to girls and go to dances. The guys
still called me Rubber Lips, but who cared anymore?"

BOB GELDOF OF THE BOOMTOWN RATS

"I'm probably the whitest singer in the world. There's
absolutely no ethnic blues sound in my voice. I have no 'soul' in the usual
sense—but I can do this great feminite falsetto that sounds just
like the way spade chicks sing."

TODD RUNDGREN

"It's strange. I spend a lot of my time
singing with Mick and Keith and I end up sounding like Dylan."

RON WOOD

"You don't always get a chance to fuck
when you're horny or punch somebody in the face when
you feel like it. . . . When people become disenchanted with the world,
they turn to fantasy—and here we are."

GENE SIMMONS OF KISS

"I sort of fancy myself as a rock & roll Columbo."

GLENN SHORROCK, LEAD VOCALIST FOR AUSTRALIA'S LITTLE RIVER BAND

"I'm sorry to say, in all fairness, you'll
never be anything. You'll never get anywhere singing in that sissy voice."

TINY TIM'S MOTHER AND FATHER

"The band liked it, so I'm as happy as a pig in shit."

JOE COCKER ON HIS TELEVISED DUET WITH COCKER MIMIC JOHN BELUSHI

"Capitalism itself in itself is a bit of a ripoff,
as far as I'm concerned, but what are you going to do?
I'm certainly not going to be a politician and change it, in or out of the
system. I'm just going to sing my songs, because that's what I do."

LEON RUSSELL

"The Grateful Dead
should be sponsored by the government—a public service. And they
should set us up to play at places that need to get high."

JERRY GARCIA

"We want to be one of the great bands, not like The Grateful Dead."

CLEM BURKE, DRUMMER FOR BLONDIE

"I think the only way we can be big in America is by accident."

ANDY PARTRIDGE OF BRITISH GROUP XTC

🌿

"You remember the fat kid at the pool
when you were little whose mother made him wear
noseplugs and earplugs and goggles and he'd have to hold them all when
he jumped in? I felt like him when the Eagles sang."

RANDY NEWMAN ON RECORDING WITH THE EAGLES

🌿

"If it weren't for the rocks in its bed, the stream would have no song."

CARL PERKINS ON THE UPS AND DOWNS OF HIS CAREER

🌿

"One day Neil Young will write
a happy song. But I'll probably sell it to TV for a commercial."

NEIL YOUNG ON HIS MUSIC

🌿

"This song has too much class
for us, but I'll be embarrassed all the way to the bank."

GEORGE CLINTON ON THE BRIDES OF FUNKENSTEIN SONG
"WHEN YOU'RE GONE"

🌿

"I thought it would be fun to play
on the Kennedy myth and culturally assassinate it."

BOSTON MUSICIAN LEE HARVEY ON HIS SINGLE "CHAP'S ACQUITTED,"
BACKED WITH "GRAY MATTER ON THE STREETS OF DALLAS"

GEORGE BURNS/photo by UPI

"Why should I write songs when Chuck Berry already wrote them all?"

GEORGE THOROGOOD

"I was fuckin' blown away.
The subtitle is 'Steal This Song.' It's obvious
to anyone with a brain the size of a LeSueur pea that it's about
Abbie Hoffman."

KINKY FRIEDMAN ON AN IMPENDING LAWSUIT FROM ABIGAIL VAN BUREN
OVER HIS SONG "DEAR ABBY"

"Damn, I look good with guns."

TED NUGENT

"Mediocrity is at such a peak right now, and I don't want to be mediocre."

SHAUN CASSIDY ON HIS CAREER

"Sometimes he shocks me,
but I have to be cool. I can't question Ike, because everything that Ike
has ever gotten me to do that I didn't like was successful."

TINA TURNER ON THEIR ACT

"The musicians I use are great.
They're all rock musicians, except they don't play too loud. They play
like they're getting paid."

GEORGE BURNS

"I can't say one album is better
than another. I never listen to them anyway."

LINDA RONSTADT ON HER MUSIC

❦

"Funk gets the shit out of your mind. Prune juice gets it out of your ass."

PARLIAMENT/FUNKADELIC'S GEORGE CLINTON, WHO GARGLES FOUR TO FIVE
QUARTS OF PRUNE JUICE A WEEK AND LIKES THE BAND TO DO THE SAME

❦

"Boar meat makes us mean,
and when the band is mean we can play some outrageous rock & roll."

TED NUGENT, WHO LIKES TO HUNT

❦

"I told him to gargle with steroids and wear a tight condom."

AEROSMITH MEMBER STEVEN TYLER'S ADVICE TO
ANOTHER SINGER WITH VOICE PROBLEMS

❦

"The last thing we worry about is taste.
We just let our media consciousness blow it out. Watching the media, you
learn to love bad taste."

FEE WAYBILL OF THE TUBES

❦

"That's a hell of an ambition,
to be mellow. It's like wanting to be senile."

RANDY NEWMAN ON MIDDLE OF THE ROAD MUSIC

"Once in a while
when I turn on the radio in the car, the lyrics I hear are really banal.
Toast—when I hear Carole King, I think of toast."

PAUL SIMON

"I don't like the word *rock* and all that shit.
Jazz is an Uncle Tom word. It's a white folks word. I never heard that shit
'til I read it in a magazine."

MILES DAVIS

"Rock & roll is one of the keys,
one of the many, many keys, to a very complex life.
Don't get fucked up with all the many keys. Groove to rock & roll and
then you'll probably find one of the best keys of all."

PETE TOWNSHEND

"Hard rock is all traditional bullshit now. . . . It's like Muzak."

STEPHEN BISHOP

"Oh, vell then, I luhv him!"

ZSA ZSA GABOR'S REACTION TO BOB DYLAN, AFTER ASKING WHO HE WAS AND
BEING TOLD THAT HE WAS "THE MOST FAMOUS ROCK STAR IN THE WORLD"

"What are Zsa Zsa Gabor and George Plimpton
and all those other society freeloaders doing at a birthday party for
Mick Jagger? If the Rolling Stones are the newest mind fuck for the
Truman Capote crowd, what does that say about the Stones?"

GRACE LICHTENSTEIN, *NEW YORK TIMES* REPORTER, LESS THAN THRILLED
AT THE SOCIAL SCENE AROUND THE STONES

"I wasn't born to the blues, man. I'm Jewish, you know;
I've been Jewish for years. Hell, man, I'm not Son House. I have not been
pissed on, stepped on, shitted on. But Butterfield is somethin' else.
There's no white bullshit from him. It wouldn't matter if he
was green. If he was a tuna fish sandwich, Butterfield
would still be into the blues."

MIKE BLOOMFIELD ON FELLOW BLUESMAN PAUL BUTTERFIELD

"After their revolution, they understand
blues too, they understand very well. Whether you be black or white, if
you're poor, you're poor."

B.B. KING ABOUT HIS RUSSIAN TOUR

"William Bonney would be more accurate.
Jesse James was motivated by greed, while Billy the Kid did it for the fun
of it. All Americans are outlaws."

JIM MORRISON ON BEING CALLED THE JESSE JAMES OF ROCK

"Goddarn! If that man can eat pussy
like he can blow harp, man, he's a motherfucker."

MUDDY WATERS ADMIRING HARP PLAYER MAGIC DICK SALWITZ OF THE J. GEILS BAND

"When I see Bachman and Fred Turner,
both 250-odd pound guys, slinking and sashaying around
onstage . . . it just doesn't work for me. It's like seeing the fuckin' hippos
in little frilly skirts on ice skates doing *Nutcracker Suite*."

BURTON CUMMINGS

"Groups like Genesis and Yes
are about as exciting as a used Kleenex. It might as well be Tony Bennett."

NICK LOWE

"When I hear the name Doobie Brothers,
and then the music they're making, I shudder. I just can't help it."

TOM JOHNSTON, EX-DOOBIE BROTHER

"I think the Sex Pistols have copped out.
Now they're on the front of *Rolling Stone*. That's a real cop-out."

MICK JAGGER

"It's a real feeling of déjâ vu.
They puked at the London airport; we pissed in the filling station."

KEITH RICHARDS ON THE SEX PISTOLS

"It's a load of bullocks,
but it's making money, and you can't argue with that."

ARIEL BENDER OF WIDOWMAKER ON THE PUNKS

"We ask them not to break too many glasses
and not to spit at somebody unless they're specifically asked. But it's
their natural aggressiveness that people want."

WILLOW MOREL, OWNER OF LONDON'S RENT-A-PUNK

"Hear it first thing
in the morning and you'd want to go straight back to bed."

ELTON JOHN ON PUNK GROUP GENERATION X

"We're still the only ones true
to the original aims of punk. Those other bands should be destroyed."

MICK JONES OF THE CLASH

"Disco is a political movement that votes with its feet."

ROBERT FRIPP, EX-LEADER OF KING CRIMSON

"Disco music is great . . . but it's an escapist's way out.
It's musical soma. Rock & roll too—it will occupy and destroy you
that way. It lets in lower elements and shadows that I don't think
are necessary. Rock has always been the devil's music."

DAVID BOWIE

"I hate disco music."

BARRY GIBB OF THE BEE GEES,

"I'm not saying this to be cool, but disco sucks—
I mean, can you imagine some kid wanting to grow up and play on a
Donna Summer album?"

LOU REED

"We're sticking our tongue in society's cheek."

DAVID HODO OF THE VILLAGE PEOPLE

"The girls are there because, well,
we're six humpy guys and they get off on the sex we're selling."

GLENN HUGHES OF THE VILLAGE PEOPLE EXPLAINING THEIR POPULARITY
WITH NONGAYS

"Who sings about
their guardian angels anymore? It's all about 'screw me, baby'."

ANGELA BOFILL

"Disco ain't Beethoven, but rock isn't as good as it thinks either."

DAVID RAPAPORT OF NEW YORK'S DISCO STATION WKTU-FM

"I'll tell you, if country & western
were the next big thing, I'd be right out there with a cowboy hat on.
That is the way of the world."

NILE RODGERS, CO-LEADER OF THE DISCO BAND CHIC

"A guy asked me about
progressive country. I told him it sucks. And not very well, at that."

DELBERT McCLINTON

"Country music is shit.
It just isn't honest any more. A cat gets out there onstage
with a fancy suit on, something made by Nudie with feathers and sequins
all over it, and he's wearin' a cowboy hat and he's from Savannah,
Georgia, man. It's phoney. How can you sell Porter Wagoner to
the kids? Nobody wants to be like Porter Wagoner."

JOE SOUTH

"I'm surprised. I didn't know musicians read books."

KURT VONNEGUT, WHEN HE FOUND THAT MEMBERS OF WILLIE NELSON'S BAND
WANTED TO MEET HIM

"I don't know if you could
call my music cowboy music. I don't sing about horses."

MERLE HAGGARD

"You don't have to have cows to be a cowboy."

NUDIE, CUSTOM WESTERN GARMENT STORE OWNER

"I feel confident and comfortable
in the L.A. studios. I'm like a kid in a toy shop, or maybe a bull in a
china closet."

BOZ SCAGGS

"This is like the Ziegfeld Follies.
No one knows what's going to happen after they enter this place."

STEVE RUBELL ON HIS NEW YORK DISCO, STUDIO 54

"The only way we made it
was with a great big old bag of Mexican reds and
two gallons of Robitussin HC. Five reds and a slug of HC and you can
sleep through anything."

BUTCH TRUCKS ON THE EARLY DAYS WHEN THE ALLMAN BROTHERS BAND
USED TO TRAVEL ELEVEN PEOPLE IN AN ECONOLINE VAN

"Those places were so tough
you had to show your razor and puke twice before they'd let you in."

RONNIE HAWKINS ON PLAYING THE HONKY-TONKS

"Maybe if I worked harder
on my guitar playing, we'd attract a better class of people."

JOE PERRY OF AEROSMITH AFTER BEING INJURED BY FLYING OBJECTS
THROWN BY FANS

"I understand that all an audience wants
is sex and violence. I know that 'cause I used to watch television all day
long. We're the ultimate American band. . . . merely the end product
of an affluent society."

ALICE COOPER

"It's the way rock seems to be going,
isn't it? After Iggy Pop and Alice Cooper, it seems the logical thing for
someone to stuff dynamite up his ass and go out with a bang."

C.P. LEE OF ALBERTO Y LOS TRIOS PARANOIAS, WHO WROTE THE WORLD'S FIRST
SNUFF-ROCK MUSICAL

"I don't think anything of it, really.
I suppose the show wasn't going too well, so Jim decided to
pull out his prick and liven it up a bit. If he likes wanking, that's okay.
I don't think he actually wanked off though; even if he did, I wish he'd
done the whole thing and fucked some bird up there.
Do the whole scene."

JOHN LENNON ON JIM MORRISON'S ARREST FOR INDECENT
EXPOSURE AT A CONCERT

"I'm still that sort to let them wet their
knickers on the seats—really. That's basically what it's about for me.'

ADAM FAITH, FORMER BRITISH POP STAR TURNED ACTOR

"The whole idea is to deliver what money can't buy."

BRUCE SPRINGSTEEN ON CONCERTS

"These people came to hear some music,
and we were trying to slip in the message at the end—like slipping a pill
in a hamburger or something."

LINDA RONSTADT SPEAKING OUT AGAINST POLITICAL FUND-RAISING CONCERTS

"You go into the Apollo, and
in every audience there's somebody out there who could
come up on stage and sing your thing better than you do. You gotta stand
on your head and whistle 'Dixie' out your ass to make them applaud."

SWAMP DOGG

"Just once I would like to persuade
the audience not to wear any article of blue denim.
If only they could see themselves in a pair of brown corduroys
like mine instead of this awful, boring blue denim. I don't
enjoy the sky or sea as much as I used to
because of this Levi character. If Jesus Christ came back today, He
and I would get into our brown corduroys and go to the nearest
jean store and overturn the racks of blue denim.
Then we'd get crucified in the morning."

IAN ANDERSON OF JETHRO TULL

BILL GRAHAM/photo by David Gahr

"It's nice to see an act whose audience can't relate to them."

LEONARD COHEN'S OPINION OF THE BAND DEVO

"Those kids don't know anything.
They're lying around in mud listening to a shitty sound system and
eating day-old garbage, and they think they're having a good time.
They're just being had, mister, had."

BILL GRAHAM ON THE "ENDLESS FESTIVAL," PRODUCED BY
SOMEONE OTHER THAN GRAHAM

"It always helps to have a few rows
of girls up front—that just makes it more rock & roll."

TOM PETTY

"I can pour beer all over everybody in the front row;
I love it, 'cause I'm a brat anyway. Pour it all over their brand new
clothes, ha ha ha. And when I throw them those dollar bills, they perform
for us—audiences are really masochists."

ALICE COOPER

"When we're onstage, we're not
vulnerable or exposed. We're up there showing off."

STEWART COPELAND, DRUMMER IN POLICE

"An English audience is like a good fuck.
You hold hands with it for a while, you kiss it, you pet it,
and then it pays you off."

GLENN FREY OF THE EAGLES

"Performing wouldn't be so bad
if everyone in the audience could come up onstage and I could kiss
them beforehand. As it is, it's like making love without any
preliminary kissing."

CARLY SIMON

"What I got kicked out
of school for, it's the same thing I see myself doing onstage now."

RICKIE LEE JONES

"Bernie and I do seem to attract weirdos. I don't know why,
because we're not really weird ourselves. People give me pineapples."

ELTON JOHN ON GROUPIES

"You ought to see our groupies.
We have the funniest groupies in the world—real bottom-of-the-barrel
stuff. We're the ugliest band ever born. When we play, I expect to find
puke in the aisles."

BLOOD, SWEAT, AND TEARS DRUMMER BOBBY COLOMBY

"We had parties that Nero would have been ashamed to attend."

RONNIE HAWKINS

"I get bored, you see. When I get bored, I rebel.
I took out me 'atchet and chopped the 'otel room to bits. The lot of it.
It happens all the time."

KEITH MOON ON HIS INFAMOUS HABIT OF
DESTROYING HOTEL ROOMS

"If you're sitting around after a show
and there's something you don't like, you just switch it off by throwing
a bottle through the screen."

KEITH MOON

"Those guys didn't belong in a motel—
they belonged in a barn out on the prairie."

MANAGER OF THE LITTLE AMERICA MOTEL IN FLAGSTAFF, ARIZONA,
AFTER WAYLON JENNINGS' ENTOURAGE LEFT

"Once there was a Woodstock; well, this is Livestock."

DAVID HILD OF THE GIRLS SURVEYING THE CROWD AT MARATHON '80
IN THE DIRT-FLOORED FIELD HOUSE OF UNIVERSITY OF MINNESOTA

"We didn't call it festival seating. We called it animal seating,
because when they came in, they came in like a herd of cattle."

AN EMPLOYEE OF CINCINNATI'S RIVERFRONT COLISEUM,
WHERE ELEVEN PEOPLE WERE TRAMPLED TO
DEATH BEFORE A WHO CONCERT

"When I got off that tour,
I remember dialing room service on my home phone."

STEVEN TYLER OF AEROSMITH ON THEIR 1977 TOUR

"I will always be ready to go.
This is not waiting to get stadium availability in Detroit. This is fucking
Russia. This is not the moon. I mean, this is bigger than the moon. There's
nobody up there to change."

BILL GRAHAM, WHO WANTS TO BRING ROCK & ROLL TO RUSSIA

"These bastards are just sucking us to death;
that's about all that we can do is do it like circus animals.
I resent being an artist in that respect; I resent performing for fucking
idiots who don't know anything."

JOHN LENNON

"They ask for an autograph but haven't got
a pen or a piece of paper. You think, 'What am I supposed to do?
Shit a miracle?'"

ELTON JOHN ON THE NUISANCE OF SOME FANS

"I think it's an honor to be asked
for an autograph, and anybody who don't think so oughta go off in the
woods and be a forest ranger so nobody'll bother him."

CHARLIE DANIELS

"I don't know whether I should play
her song now—this could create a whole new approach to promotion."

PAUL DREW, RKO RADIO VICE-PRESIDENT OF PROGRAMMING, AFTER BEING
HIT IN THE EYE BY BETTE MIDLER WHEN HE TOLD HER HE DIDN'T LIKE
HER NEW RECORD

"I would like to know by what right
these 'eyes of blue, ears of tin' have the right to criticize or canonize,
or fault or praise anybody. Some of them admitted to me they
can't even hear the music."

JERRY WEXLER ON ROCK CRITICS

JOHN LENNON, RINGO STARR, GEORGE HARRISON, PAUL McCARTNEY/photo by Movie Star News

"I am convinced they are descendants
of Attila the Hun, Hitler, and Charles Manson."

FRANK SINATRA ON CRITICS

"I bet he's about four foot three.
I bet he's got boogies up his nose. I bet his feet smell."

ELTON JOHN REACTING TO BEING PANNED BY *NEW YORK TIMES*
CRITIC JOHN ROCKWELL

"It's obvious he doesn't understand our music.
He oughta stick to the familiar stuff like the Ice Capades,
Water Follies, and the pantyhose boys."

CHARLIE DANIELS OBJECTING TO A REVIEW COMPARING HIS BAND
TO THE ALLMAN BROTHERS

"They insist on painting me as this tragic . . .
well, not even a tragic, because in this town people don't understand
tragedy. All they understand is drama. You have to be *moral* to
understand tragedy."

JONI MITCHELL ON BAD REVIEWS

"Can you imagine working for a fucking year,
and you get a B-plus from an asshole in the *Village Voice*?"

LOU REED ON A REVIEW OF HIS ALBUM *TAKE NO PRISONERS*

"Tell Dave I'm not upset
and I'll be happy to sell him an album this year to review."

STEVE MARTIN'S COMMENT ON AN UNFAVORABLE REVIEW BY DAVE MARSH

"It's like a soup that's out there
for three weeks, and you open it and these maggots come out."

BILL GRAHAM'S CRITICISM OF THE FIRST ROCK MUSIC AWARDS

"You get criticized
when you do something new and innovative. To me it was superheavy."

DON KIRSHNER REACTING TO CRITICISM OF HIS ROCK MUSIC AWARDS

"Rock & roll does not belong in a tuxedo.
When I saw them walk out there, my fuckin' heart sank. It was like the
end of an era."

GLENN FREY ON SEEING CROSBY, STILLS, AND NASH IN FORMAL ATTIRE
AT THE GRAMMYS

"After they hear me sing
'Fast Buck Freddie,' they'll probably take it back."

GRACE SLICK ON SPECULATION THAT SHE WOULD WIN A ROCK MUSIC AWARD

"So many people have had reservations
about this company of ours, we decided to put the crow
on our album and the labels. That crow's for eating. Either we or a lot of
other people are going to have to eat that crow."

RON RAKOW, PRESIDENT OF GRATEFUL DEAD RECORDS

"It's the only company I know
that gives you a manual of where to go after gigs: nightclubs, bars, and the
local venereal disease clinic, which can't be bad, can it?"

THIN LIZZY'S PHIL LYNOTT ON THEIR SWITCH TO WARNER BROS.

JAMES TAYLOR/photo by David Gahr

"The next cover I make, I'll get someone with an airbrush,
I'll get a tan on my ass, and I'll get someone to photograph it with one of
those lights that makes a halo around you, and I'll call it 'James Taylor—
Like You Like Him'."

JAMES TAYLOR ON PLEASING THE PUBLIC

"As soon as you start talking about mystique, you have none.
After all, it's just me and Frank Sinatra left on Reprise Records."

NEIL YOUNG

"I'd rather the Mafia than Decca."

KEITH RICHARDS' ANGER THAT DECCA PUT MONEY MADE BY THE STONES
INTO THE COMPANY'S RADAR DIVISION, WHICH MADE PARTS
FOR AIR FORCE BOMBERS FOR VIETNAM

"We know where the kids are at, man,
because we deal with them all the time. These fuckers don't even know
where their own kids are at."

JOHN SINCLAIR, MANAGER OF THE MC5, ON THAT BAND'S RIFT WITH ELEKTRA

"We're insulted that we haven't been dropped. Who wants
to be on a label where the president quotes Spiro Agnew to you?"

SIMON STOKES AND HIS BLACK WHIP THRILL BAND ON THEIR RECORD COMPANY,
MGM, AND ITS PRESIDENT, MIKE CURB

"We used to have to carry the Arkansas credit card—
a syphon hose and a five-gallon can. I was the only rock & roll singer who
performed every night with chafed lips."

RONNIE HAWKINS ON HIS BAND'S HUMBLE BEGINNINGS

"I don't know if dissatisfied
is the right word; disgusted is more like it. It's like Captive Records. We
used to call them Captive Records instead of Capitol."

BEACH BOYS' MIKE LOVE AND BRUCE JOHNSTON ON THEIR EX-RECORD COMPANY

"I look at songs like real estate.
A song is like a building. It's an annuity on which
you collect residuals. But I'm in the music business rather than stocks
because I love talent and I love music. It's the essence of our culture."

DON KIRSHNER

"We don't want to censor your songs.
What we want to do is change your song. You're the younger generation;
you believe in change."

PAUL KANTNER QUOTING RCA RECORDS PRESIDENT
ROCCO LAGINESTRA

"I buy Mobil gas. I might as well
make a record through another big corporation."

PETE SEEGER ON HIS NEW ALBUM FOR WARNER BROS.

"I took a switch-blade out of my boot
and started admiring the edge. Then we made headway."

TOM PETTY ON NEGOTIATING HIS CONTRACT

"If Patty Hearst were on
United Artists Records she never would have been found."

DEAN TORRENCE OF JAN AND DEAN

"Sure I lie, but it's more like . . . tinting."

ROCK MANAGER IRVING AZOFF

🌱

"I can't claim any contribution to their songwriting.
I wish I could. I'd be taking their royalties, I assure you."

ROBERT STIGWOOD ON THE BEE GEES' SONGS

🌱

"It's hard to say you're happy with your balls sewn shut in your mouth."

WARREN ZEVON, LIKENING HIS CURRENT ARTISTIC SITUATION TO THE
CLASSIC FATE OF LUCKLESS SMUGGLERS

🌱

"The era of throwing albums against the wall to see if they stick is over."

MERCURY-PHONOGRAM PRESIDENT ROBERT SHERWOOD TALKING ABOUT
HARD TIMES IN THE RECORD INDUSTRY

🌱

"When an individual with as much perception as myself
decides to honor those pipsqueaks by recording them instead of pissing on
them, the first thing they should do is kneel and kiss his ass."

DOUG WESTON, OWNER OF LOS ANGELES' TROUBADOUR CLUB, ACCUSED OF
TAPING BANDS WITHOUT THEIR PERMISSION

🌱

"I think the music business is full of shit.
My favorite people are nobody. I don't like anybody.
I don't like anything. I hate everything except I love rock & roll,
and the people who work for me are the greatest people in the world."

PRODUCER MIKE CHAPMAN

"This is the best point of my life I'm living
right now. I'm glad it came before I died, I can tell you. Feels great."

MUDDY WATERS ON ACHIEVING COMMERCIAL SUCCESS

"It looks exciting but it ain't nothing. It's what you call show business."

DIZZY GILLESPIE

"Ah just love bein' famous and ah think
anybody who says they don't is full of shit."

JOHNNY WINTER

"Success always necessitates a degree of ruthlessness.
Given the choice of friendship or success, I'd probably choose success."

STING, LEAD SINGER OF THE POLICE

"Sometimes I feel like a kid
having the first Christmas he can remember. You know, Alice in Wonderland
and all that. It's unbelievable."

B.B. KING ON HIS SUCCESS

"I don't like to be driven. Except wild."

PAUL McCARTNEY ON DRIVING

"If you're in a limmie,
you could be Mickey Mouse and you'd be waved through to the front."

SINGER RUTH COPELAND ON THE MERITS OF THE LIMOUSINE

"We believe in keeping the glamour
in show business, and that's why we wear suits onstage.
You've got to look smart. If you walk out onstage and look like
one of the audience, the mystique is gone. They pay to be entertained,
and you've got to give them a show for their money. You're supposed
to be unreal. . . . We drive Rolls-Royces. People see someone in a
Rolls-Royce and they want one too. They want to make it.
If you don't have people in Rolls-Royces, then you don't
have anyone trying to get one. Nobody wants to hit any
heights or earn anything. You've got no business."

THE BEE GEES IN 1971

"Being a survivor, I think, of contemporary music is an accomplishment."

ROY ORBISON

"Listening to these records every night
is great, but it can turn into mental masturbation after a while."

DJ TOM DONAHUE ON LEAVING KSAN-FM

"The Golden Age of rock was yesterday."

ROCK PROMOTER BILL GRAHAM IN 1974

"I've always seen David as a building.
I visualize him as a building. Something rather like the Pan Am Building
on Park Avenue."

TONY DeFRIES, DAVID BOWIE'S MANAGER

"He's a little too fairyish looking for me. I guess
it's because I'm American, but I don't like to see boys wearing makeup."

PATTI SMITH ON DAVID BOWIE

"I feel as if I've been shitting
without eating, intellectually. I'm just all shit and no food. So what I'm
going to do is eat through my brain—feed my head,
as a matter of fact."

GRACE SLICK ON QUITTING JEFFERSON STARSHIP

"I want out of this rock & roll circus."

STEPHEN STILLS IN 1973

"Dey da heaviest act in the business. Do ya understan'?
If Jesus Christ came to town, he wouldn't sell more tickets."

WOLFMAN JACK ON THE ROLLING STONES

"I think Mick Jagger would be astounded and amazed if he
realized to how many people he is not a sex symbol but a mother image."

DAVID BOWIE

"He moves like a parody between a majorette girl and Fred Astaire."

TRUMAN CAPOTE ON MICK JAGGER

"It's a bit like having an orgasm.
Sometimes an orgasm is better than being onstage;
sometimes being onstage is better than having an orgasm."

MICK JAGGER ON HIS WORK

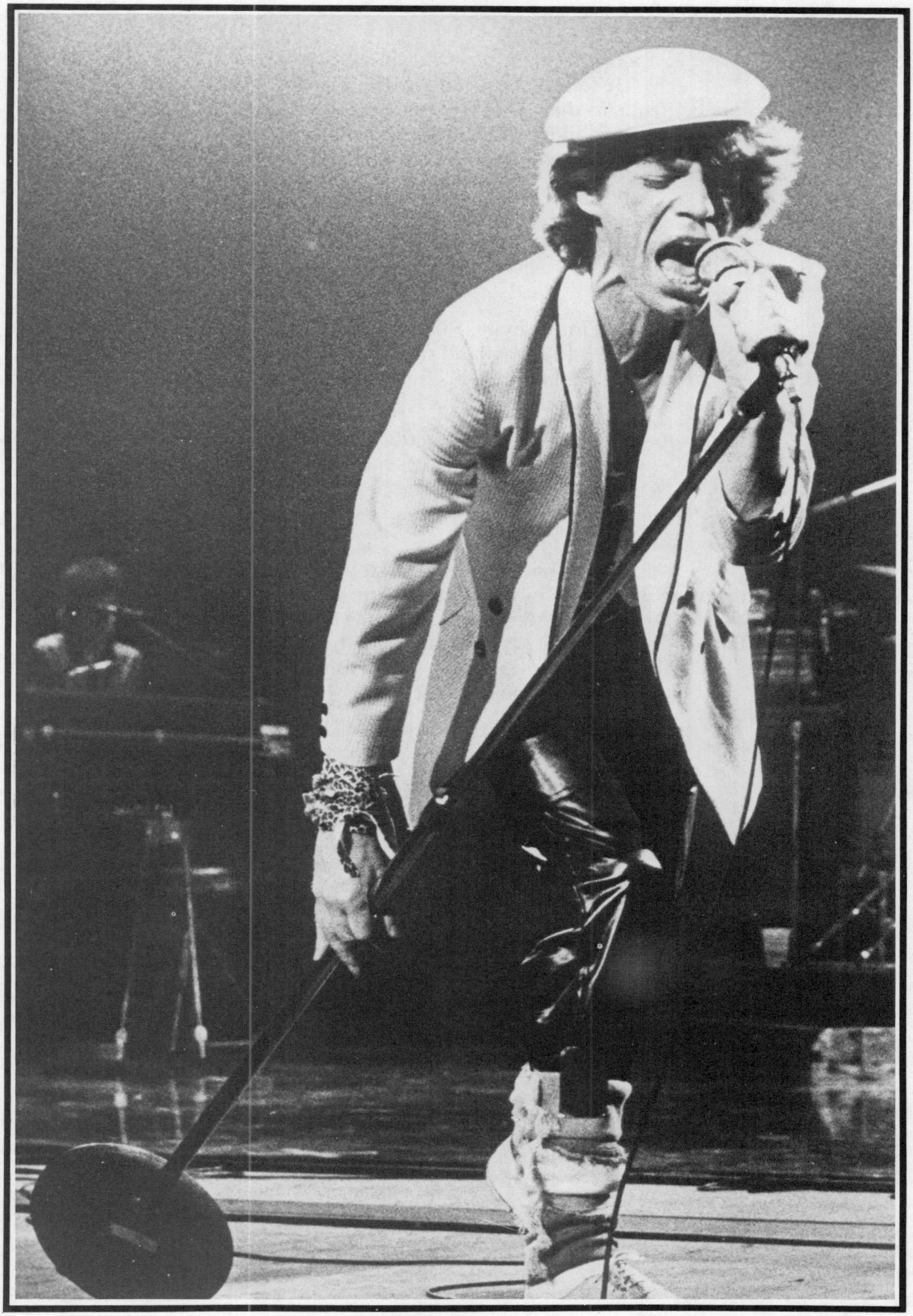

MICK JAGGER OF THE ROLLING STONES/photo by UPI

"He's stoned on himself. He's always
in complete control and the whole thing is manipulation. It really bothers
me that a twerp like that can parade around and convince
everybody that he's Satan."

RY COODER'S ASSESSMENT OF MICK JAGGER

"I think it's a lot of hype. I like 'Honky Tonk Women'
but I think Mick's a joke, with all that fag dancing; I always did.
I enjoy it, I'll probably go and see his films and all, like everybody else,
but really, I think it's a joke."

JOHN LENNON'S OPINION OF THE STONES IN 1971.

"Jagger has got this marvelous sense
of the day in which a family breaks up. The son throws acid in the
mother's face, the mother stomps the son's nuts in and then the
fat cousin comes and says, what is everybody fighting for,
let's have dinner. And they sit down. . . .
British family life continues."

NORMAN MAILER, TALKING ABOUT MICK JAGGER

"He's not unlike Elton John,
who represents the token queen—like Liberace used to. He represents
the sort of harmless, bourgeois kind of evil that one can
accept with a shrug."

DAVID BOWIE ON MICK JAGGER

"I certainly don't want to go onstage and
just stand there like Scott Walker and be ever so pretentious. I can't
hardly sing, you know what I mean? I'm no Tom Jones and I
couldn't give a fuck."

MICK JAGGER ON THE ACROBATICS OF HIS ACT

"I'm a dedicated show-business person. I'll go onstage and do Noel Coward.''

MICK JAGGER

"Because we couldn't remember their fucking names.''

KEITH RICHARDS' REPLY WHEN ASKED WHY THE ROLLING STONES CALLED
THEIR ALBUM *SOME GIRLS*

"I refused to drop 'Some Girls.'
I've always said, if you can't take a joke, it's too fucking bad.''

MICK JAGGER ON CRITICISM OF THAT SONG'S DESCRIPTION OF WOMEN
OF DIFFERENT RACES AND NATIONALITIES

"Any bright girl would understand that if I were gay, I'd say
the same things about guys. Sometimes I do say nice things about girls.''

MICK JAGGER, REPLYING TO CRITICISM THAT HIS LYRICS
WERE NEGATIVE TO WOMEN

"I don't know why I wrote it.
Maybe I came out of the closet. It's about an imaginary person who comes
from L.A. to New York and becomes a garbage collector.''

MICK JAGGER ON THE SONG "WHEN THE WHIP COMES DOWN"

"Nine months of listening
to the Rolling Stones is not my idea of heaven.''

MICK JAGGER AFTER COMPLETING *LOVE YOU LIVE*

KEITH RICHARDS OF THE ROLLING STONES/*photo by Chuck Pulin*

**"I don't think *Sticky Fingers*
is a heavy drug album any more than the world is a heavy world."**

KEITH RICHARDS

**"That's like illiterate people complaining
they're being discriminated against because a program has words on it
and they can't read."**

MICK JAGGER RESPONDING TO PROTESTS FROM A BLIND GROUP
THAT A BRAILLE PROGRAM FOR THEIR BENEFIT CONCERT WAS PATRONIZING

"Ray Charles is nothing but a blind, ignorant nigger."

ELVIS COSTELLO

"Joni Mitchell is about as modest as Mussolini."

DAVID CROSBY

**"They said I hated Jimmy McCullough's guts.
What I really said is that he's a nasty little cunt. There's a big difference,
you know."**

GEOFF BRITTEN, FORMER WINGS DRUMMER, CLAIMING HE WAS MISQUOTED
IN *MELODY MAKER*

**"I said that I didn't think Chevy Chase could ad-lib a fart after
a baked-bean dinner. I think he took umbrage at that a little bit."**

JOHNNY CARSON

"He can get both feet, both hands,
and his hat in his mouth at the same time."

SENATOR BARRY GOLDWATER ON UN AMBASSADOR ANDREW YOUNG

"You may think bad of Wilbur Mills,
but at least old Wilbur got his girlfriend out of the water—and there's
not a Kennedy in Massachusetts who can say that."

FORMER CONGRESSMAN JOHN RARICK IN 1975

"No president in history has been more vilified
or was more vilified during the time he was President than Lincoln.
Those who knew him, his secretaries, have written that he was deeply
hurt by what was said about him and drawn about him, but on the other
hand, Lincoln had the great strength of character never to display it,
always to stand tall and strong and firm no matter how harsh or
unfair the criticism might be. These elements of greatness,
of course, inspire us all today."

RICHARD NIXON

"I remember passing Richard Nixon
in the Bel Air Hotel. Man, he was so wooden, so lifeless, it was like passing
a cigar-store Indian. Or maybe the highest art of the mortician."

ROBERT REDFORD

"Nixon—I guess I'm just not in his audience.
I believe Ralph Williams more than I believe Nixon."

LEON RUSSELL REFERRING TO A WELL-KNOWN USED CAR DEALER
ON THE WEST COAST

"Peron is our leader because he has taught us
to live like machos in a world of cowardly fairies. We are going to crush
the Leftists because Peron has ordered it. . . . I will be by him even if he
orders me to clean latrines."

JUAN MUCIACCIA, SECRETARY GENERAL OF THE RIGHT-WING
PERONIST YOUTH MOVEMENT IN MARCH, 1974

❧

"While the specter of Chairperson Bryant
astride a galloping white horse as a kind of Ginny Orangeseed
spreading bigotry throughout the land is certainly theatrical enough,
the woman is dangerous."

ROD McKUEN ON ANITA BRYANT'S CRUSADE AGAINST HOMOSEXUALS

❧

"She was wearing organdy and stuff.
She rustled when she walked by like a fucking redwood. She had big fat
earrings and was perfumed to the gills."

HOWIE KAYLAN, TURTLES LEAD SINGER,
DESCRIBING TRICIA NIXON AT A PARTY

❧

"Rockefeller is the greatest symbol
of what's wrong with this country: concentrated wealth and power,
intervention in other countries' affairs and a wasteful military budget."

PRESIDENTIAL CANDIDATE FRED HARRIS IN 1975

❧

"I do believe in the lesser
of two evils, and in that spirit I became a McGovern supporter."

ART GARFUNKEL

❧

"Do you believe I am the best-dressed
statesman of 1977? Humphrey called me and said, 'I don't believe it.' "

VICE PRESIDENT WALTER MONDALE

"Mondale is a 100 percent bona fide liberal.
It gives us a tangible target. We're not just running against this peanut
farmer who walks on water."

PETER F. KAYE, A FORD CAMPAIGN SPOKESMAN, IN 1976

"What you'll have here that day
is a man who has been trained and educated all his life to become ruler
of Britain talking with a guy who'd like to be ruler of the U.S."

B.T. COLLINS, AIDE TO CALIFORNIA GOVERNOR JERRY BROWN, DISCUSSING AN
UPCOMING MEETING BETWEEN BROWN AND PRINCE CHARLES

" I think Jerry [Brown] needs people around
who'll say, 'No,' who'll say, 'That's wrong.' The whole thing is repulsive
to me—that people want to get close to the throne, be right next
to Jerry Brown. Yecch!"

DONALD BURNS, BROWN'S LONGTIME FRIEND AND DEPARTING SECRETARY OF
BUSINESS AND TRANSPORTATION FOR CALIFORNIA

"I consider Doonesbury one of my key political advisers."

JERRY BROWN, WHEN ASKED IF HE FOUND GARY TRUDEAU'S *DOONESBURY*
CARTOONS OF HIM DEFAMATORY

"It's always an honor to be introduced by Hubert Humphrey.
In the Senate we have been an effective team: Hubert
supplies the eloquence and I supply the charisma."

SENATOR HENRY "SCOOP" JACKSON

"He's a very nice fellow,
but that's not enough, gentlemen. So's my Uncle Fred."

HUBERT HUMPHREY ON GERALD FORD

"He took a little from Dean Rusk,
a little from William Westmoreland, and a little from Custer."

FRED HARRIS ON PRESIDENT FORD'S STATE OF THE WORLD SPEECH IN 1975

"Only Gerald Ford could make a trip
to Peking, China, seem like a trip to Pekin, Illinois."

A MEMBER OF FORD'S PARTY TRAVELING TO CHINA

"It troubles me that he [Ford] played center
on the football team. That means he can only consider options for the
twenty yards in either direction, and that he has spent a good deal
of his life looking at the world upside down through his legs."

MARTIN PERETZ, EDITORIAL DIRECTOR AT *NEW REPUBLIC*

"They are both dedicated Americans
who believe in the basic values of the country—
distinguished citizens and good friends of mine. . . . They happen to be of
different parties and make slightly different appeals to people, but
that's part of our system."

VICE PRESIDENT NELSON ROCKEFELLER, COMPARING PRESIDENT FORD
TO GEORGE WALLACE

"I tell you, though, I'd dig to meet Wallace.
The governor. Yeah, I bet he's a gas, man, behind his game."

KEITH RICHARDS

"Reagan's the kind of guy who requests 'Melancholy Baby'—sober."

GEORGE MURPHY, *SAN FRANCISCO CHRONICLE* REPORTER

"Elvis is still the myth to beat—what in essence
is America. I used to have a hunch that Wallace was going to pick Elvis
as his running mate. If he'd done that I think he would have picked up
five more states. Most people would pick Elvis over Reagan. I would."

PHIL OCHS

"I find intellectuals are more interested in gossip
than anybody else—Arthur Schlesinger is the biggest gossip in the world."

DOROTHY SCHIFF, PUBLISHER OF THE *NEW YORK POST*, 1976

"People ask me who my heroes are. I have only one—Hitler.
I admire Hitler because he pulled his country together when it
was in a terrible state in the early Thirties. But the situation here is
so desperate now that one man would not be enough. We need four or
five Hitlers in Vietnam."

NGUYEN CAO KY, PREMIER OF SOUTH VIETNAM, IN 1965

"The truth is, there have never been
very many remarkable people around at any one time. Most are always
leaning on the guy next to them, asking him what to do."

WOODY ALLEN

"Where does that pompous creep come off
bad-mouthing me like that when he never even met me
and probably hasn't even seen my act? . . . Just for that I'm
gonna stick around in this business just long enough to piss on
John Denver's flowers!"

ALICE COOPER, REPLYING TO JOHN DENVER'S ASSERTION THAT HE
WOULD BE AROUND WHEN ALICE WAS LONG FORGOTTEN

"It's just like a cheap Japanese horror movie."

MANAGER SHEP GORDON, ASSESSING ALICE COOPER'S SHOW

"I can imagine him becoming a successful
hairdresser, a singing Vidal Sassoon."

MALCOLM McLAREN, JOHNNY ROTTEN'S FORMER MANAGER, ON ROTTEN'S CAREER

"Well, he beat out Keith Richards for the story of the year."

GUITARIST JOHNNY THUNDERS, COMMENTING ON SID VICIOUS' ARREST
FOR MURDER IN CONNECTION WITH THE SLAYING
OF HIS GIRLFRIEND

"It must have been really incredible
to have been good-looking, a poet, and be straight."

LOU REED ON THE LATE DELMORE SCHWARTZ

"That's the Jesus coat Bob Dylan gave me.
He bought it at Nudie's. That was before he was born again—fucker
probably wants it back now."

KINKY FRIEDMAN

"My wife gets more exercise
from shuddering than from picking up the baby."

WARREN ZEVON ON HIS PENCHANT FOR PUNNING

"The first time I saw Rickie Lee, she reminded me
of Jayne Mansfield. . . . Her style onstage was appealing and arousing,
sorta like that of a sexy white spade."

TOM WAITS ON RICKIE LEE JONES

"When she sings 'Dr. Feelgood,'
that's where she's at. The Supremes are the other thing, you know;
they're the urban Negro, airline stewardesses, or something
like the Kim sisters."

MIKE BLOOMFIELD ON ARETHA FRANKLIN

"Buddy is Superspade.
If you melted down James Brown and Arthur Conley and Otis Redding
into one enormous spade, you'd have Buddy."

MIKE BLOOMFIELD ON BUDDY MILES

" 'The Killer.' I could kill more people
with one fucking finger than he did when I saw him. I find rock & roll acts
like that pathetic now. . . . Chuck Berry is God, but what the fuck has
he written?"

ELTON JOHN ON JERRY LEE LEWIS, A.K.A. "THE KILLER"

"I thought Brian was a perfect gentleman,
apart from buttering his head and trying to put it between
two slices of bread."

TOM PETTY'S ASSESSMENT OF THE BEACH BOYS' BRIAN WILSON
AT A LOS ANGELES RESTAURANT

"I never met him but I expect to see him in heaven.
He was deeply religious, especially during the last two years of his life."

BILLY GRAHAM ON ELVIS PRESLEY

"Mao? Mao! You are, yes, . . . the Mao Zedong of rock.
The people's promoter, you are, Bill, yes. . . . But now you're a film star,
too, like Jackie Gleason or Bob Eubanks. Only you're different. . . .
You made a million dollars before you won your Oscar."

PETER RUDGE, MANAGER OF THE ROLLING STONES, TALKING TO
BILL GRAHAM IN 1972

"Well, he's skinny and bald."

BLUE THUMB RECORDS HEAD BOB KRASNOW, ASKED TO COMMENT ON CLIVE DAVIS

"The man bears a striking resemblance to a Jewish Dennis the Menace."

GLENN FREY OF THE EAGLES, ON MANAGER IRVING AZOFF

"I thought they called him Omelet
'cause he liked to eat omelets, the way they might call a cat Hamhocks
who eats hamhocks."

OTIS REDDING, WHEN CORRECTED IN REFERENCE TO ATLANTIC RECORDS
PRESIDENT AHMET ERTEGUN

"If only these guys could write as well as they play."

MICK JAGGER, ASSESSING THE *ROLLING STONE* MAGAZINE STAFF BAND

"He is a pelvic missionary.
He's laid more ugly women than you'd ever believe. Ali wants
to be liked. He has a great capacity to give and receive, and it carries over
into exchanging bodies. He thinks the woman will remember it
all her life."

MUHAMMAD ALI'S PERSONAL PHYSICIAN, DR. FERNANDO PACHECO

"Ernest Hemingway: when his cock wouldn't stand up, he blew his head off. He sold himself a line of bullshit and bought it."

FEMINIST GERMAINE GREER

"I know people theorize that Mick thought it would be amusing to marry his twin. But actually he wanted to achieve the ultimate by making love to himself."

BIANCA JAGGER, AS ATTRIBUTED BY THE *NATIONAL STAR*

"Jagger and Lennon show you that living an ordinary life is only boring."

ELTON JOHN

"I'd like to see John Lennon play Trotsky in a film."

JEAN-LUC GODARD, FRENCH FILMMAKER

"Paul is climbing Everest because it's the only mountain in the area that he can pronounce."

GRACE SLICK ON FELLOW STARSHIP MEMBER PAUL KANTNER

"My feelings toward Christ are that he was a bloody good bloke, even though he wasn't as funny as Margaret Thatcher."

TERRY JONES, DIRECTOR OF THE MONTY PYTHON FILM *LIFE OF BRIAN*

"You mean you actually can spend $70,000 at Woolworth's?"

BOB KRASNOW OF BLUE THUMB RECORDS, AFTER SEEING
IKE AND TINA TURNER'S HOUSE

"Only Tammy Wynette and Alice Cooper
know how hard it is to be a woman."

ALICE COOPER ON THE LYRICS TO HIS SONG "ONLY WOMEN BLEED"

"The Congress passed it,
the president signed it, and I guess they know more about women
than I do."

GENERAL OMAR BRADLEY ON THE ADMISSION OF WOMEN TO WEST POINT

"I want to turn women loose on the environmental
crisis. . . . Nobody knows more about pollution when detergents
back up in the kitchen sink."

NELSON ROCKEFELLER

"No, but if she were a boy, I might be."

PAT BOONE, WHEN ASKED IF HE IS JEALOUS OF HIS DAUGHTER'S SUCCESS

"I don't believe I could have chosen a woman
to be vice-president who cares more about day-care centers, care for the
deprived, and women's rights than Fritz Mondale."

JIMMY CARTER

"He seems like a very nice fella to me. Oh, 'scuze me.
It's a woman. Ain't nothing wrong with that."

JERRY LEE LEWIS, INTRODUCING A KENTUKY GUBERNATORIAL CANDIDATE

"As a matter of fact, Nancy never had any
interest in politics or anything else when we got married."

RONALD REAGAN ON HIS WIFE

"In horse vernacular, Roy has always
'given me my head' and I have tried to do the same for him."

DALE EVANS

"I'm like a woman because I have my periods,
if you know what I mean. Every once in a while I get the cramps and do
something far out."

CAPTAIN BEEFHEART

"Most gentlemen, thank heavens, still
open doors for women, which I happen to like.
We've worked out a number of accommodations; now the
head of state and I go through the doors side by side. If it's a
narrower door, we sort of sidle through it sideways."

SHIRLEY TEMPLE BLACK, U.S. CHIEF OF PROTOCOL, 1976

"I've been a woman for
nearly sixty-two years. I really don't think about it too much."

DIXY LEE RAY, GOVERNOR OF WASHINGTON, 1976

"I love being a woman.
You can cry. You get to wear
pants now. If you're on a boat and it's
going to sink, you get to go on the rescue boat first.
You get to wear cute clothes. It must be a great thing,
or so many men wouldn't be wanting to do it now."

GILDA RADNER

"It would be difficult for me to say I'm against
working women when I've had a Champagne Lady on my show for
nineteen years. . . . I like clean ladies and nice ladies."

LAWRENCE WELK

"That criticism comes from people
who think that women should be karate
instructors or airplane pilots. I'm not knocking that everyone
should achieve what she wants to achieve—but when a man's looking
for a woman, he ain't looking for a woman who's an airplane pilot. He's
looking for a woman to help him out and support him, to hold up
one end while he holds up the other."

BOB DYLAN ON ACCUSATIONS THAT HE IS A CHAUVINIST

"I would not want a woman flying on my wing
because I would be just naturally more interested in her safety than my
own or the objective of hitting the enemy, and the chances are
I would get clobbered. So, I want them back
where they belong."

SENATOR BARRY GOLDWATER ON LEGISLATION TO OPEN NEW
MILITARY POSITIONS TO WOMEN

"I don't care how some women feel about it,
but I would hate to see the nation rely on women for our combat forces."

RONALD REAGAN

"They're asking women to do impossible
things. I don't believe women can carry a pack, live in
a foxhole, or go a week without a bath."

GENERAL WILLIAM WESTMORELAND ON WOMEN IN THE ARMED SERVICES

"Women are important in a man's life only
if they're beautiful and charming and keep their femininity. This business
of feminism, for instance. . . . You're equal in the eyes of the law,
but not—excuse my saying so—in intelligence."

MOHAMMED RIZA PAHLEVI, FORMER SHAH OF IRAN

"They should be liberated if they want to be—
just like the blacks. Should we give them all their rights? I think they
should have them, yes. . . . While they have them, make them
feel a little inferior."

MARVIN GAYE ON WOMEN'S RIGHTS

"We're living in an age where
you have to call a chick and ask her if she'll wear
a dress tonight. And they say, 'You're weird.' "

SINGER/SONGWRITER TIM ROSE

"When I was already in Los Angeles
in my pink Cadillac, they were just three years old, and now I go out
with them. It feels all right."

MICK JAGGER ON YOUNGER WOMEN

"At my concerts most of the chicks
are looking for liberation; they think I'm gonna show 'em
how to do it. But the ones right in front are always the country club
bitches; they always are. It's so weird playing to fourteen panty girdles."

JANIS JOPLIN

"Fucking groupies. I'm telling you,
the next one who pushes herself at me, I'm going to
piss all over her. . . . Wait till me mother reads that; she'll never speak to
me again."

OZZY OSBOURNE, OF BLACK SABBATH

"You get to ball the prettiest boys . . .
smoke the best dope . . . meet all the most far-out people."

PATTI CAKES ON BEING A GROUPIE IN 1970

"Nobody can argue any longer
about the rights of women. It's like arguing about earthquakes."

AUTHOR LILLIAN HELLMAN

"This could be the social disease of the future.
What I'm treating now may only be the tip of the iceberg."

TOM DURKIN, SOCIAL WORKER, EXPLAINING THAT WOMEN'S DEMANDS FOR EQUAL
TREATMENT ARE LEADING TO AN INCREASE IN MALE IMPOTENCE

"No one is going to take women's liberation seriously
until women recognize that they will not be thought of as equals in the
secret privacy of men's most private mental parts
until they eschew alimony."

NORMAN MAILER

"Give me two weeks in any capital city
and some good-looking women, and I'll deliver the ERA on a platter."

MARGO ST. JAMES, FOUNDER OF COYOTE, THE NATIONAL
HOOKERS' RIGHTS LOBBY

"If I'm going to play chess,
I don't think I should play it differently because I'm a woman."

WRITER-CRITIC SUSAN SONTAG ON FEMINISM

"I hate Ms. There really isn't anything
like making small battles in order to lose big ones. That's what the whole
women's movement has been about to me."

LILLIAN HELLMAN

"I don't mind sharing a bathroom
with a lady. It doesn't scare the shit out of me, you know what I mean?"

JON VOIGHT ON BEING A FEMINIST

"I think she's got a lot of style, but no breasts."

TRUMAN CAPOTE ON BIANCA JAGGER

"I like Bianca Jagger
because she is one of the few women I know who has as much class and
style as I have."

BRITT EKLAND, SWEDISH ACTRESS

"If I don't feel like wearing a bra,
I don't wear one. I'd never let my nipples show at a state function, though.
I'd be frightened the old men would have heart attacks."

MARGARET TRUDEAU, WIFE OF CANADIAN PRIME MINISTER
PIERRE TRUDEAU, 1977

"The one on my tit is for me and my friends.
Just a little treat for the boys, like icing on the cake."

JANIS JOPLIN ON HER TATTOOS

"Stella [Parton] is flat-chested."

BILLY CARTER

"At least my situation can be remedied,
but who ever heard of silicone for the brain?"

STELLA PARTON, DOLLY'S SISTER

"I would love to change the bunny outfit
to something more contemporary. I don't think a girl needs to have big
boobs to be attractive anymore, and I think it would be a lot
sexier to be served by someone in, maybe,
a little see-through T-shirt."

BARBI BENTON

"A pair of tits like that
and you tend to forget that she has a voice—but she sounds incredible."

BARBI BENTON'S PRODUCER, ROGER GLOVER

"I'll make two predictions: big bands will not
come back, and Dolly Parton will continue to be the only girl singer
with big tits to sell records."

ARTIE MOGULL, PRESIDENT OF UNITED ARTISTS RECORDS

"Sophia Loren is the embodiment of what
a woman should be—the epitome of femaleness. Most of the young
people today are just ironing boards."

RONA BARRETT

"Nobody can be the most beautiful girl
in the world. It's just fairy-tale time."

RAQUEL WELCH

"We all know that most women are built like pears."

JERRY SILVERMAN, DRESS COMPANY PRESIDENT

"Women do seem to be by nature more inclined
to be monogamous. I'm going to incur the wrath of every women's
rights person, but I just think that that's more of a natural inclination."

LINDA RONSTADT

"A southern girl gets a lot of quiet time
to think about being female. And when you're not allowed to do certain
things, you get more interested in them. I mean, you know something
must be awful good if you're not supposed to do it until
the last minute."

DOLLY PARTON

"The big mistake that men make is that
when they turn thirteen or fourteen, and all of a sudden they've
reached puberty, they believe that they like women. Actually, you're
just horny. It doesn't mean that you like women any more at twenty-one
than you did at ten."

JULES FEIFFER, CARTOONIST

"I've always been the one to push and shove
and say, 'Sorry, that's it darlin', it's all over, goodbye. Take twenty
Valiums and have a stomach pump and that's the end of it.' "

ROD STEWART

"Life isn't fair."

PRESIDENT JIMMY CARTER, JUSTIFYING HIS OPPOSITION TO
FEDERAL FUNDING OF ABORTIONS

"Pregnancy is of course confined to women,
but it is in other ways significantly different from the typical covered
disease or disability."

JUSTICE WILLIAM H. REHNQUIST, DEFENDING THE 1976 SUPREME COURT
DECISION THAT EMPLOYERS WERE NOT REQUIRED TO PROVIDE
PREGNANCY BENEFITS

"Boys were hanging around the girls,
and sterilization was the most convenient method to prevent pregnancy."

SPOKESPERSON FOR A FEDERALLY FUNDED FAMILY-PLANNING CLINIC IN
MONTGOMERY, ALABAMA, AFTER STERILIZING TWO BLACK GIRLS
AGED TWELVE AND FOURTEEN

"Y'know the problem with men? After the birth, we're irrelevant."

DUSTIN HOFFMAN, DISCUSSING NATURAL CHILDBIRTH

"I personally can't think of anything
more aggressive than actually sticking something into someone."

GRAHAM HILL, RACE DRIVER, ARGUING THAT WOMEN ARE NOT
BIOLOGICALLY AGGRESSIVE ENOUGH TO CHALLENGE MALE DRIVERS

"I'd rather give head to a beautiful woman
than fuck her, really. I'm just another chick, I'm a lesbian chick."

DENNIS HOPPER, ACTOR

"Human beings are not animals, and I do not
want to see sex and sexual differences treated as casually and as amorally
as dogs and other beasts treat them. I believe this could happen
under the ERA."

RONALD REAGAN

"How are you? Did you do any fornicating this weekend?"

RICHARD NIXON TO DAVID FROST

"It's just as Christian
to get down on your knees for sex as it is for religion."

LARRY FLYNT, PUBLISHER OF *HUSTLER*

"Sex without class consciousness
cannot give satisfaction, even if it is repeated until infinity."

ALDO BRANDIRALI, 1973 SECRETARY-GENERAL OF THE ITALIAN
MARXIST-LENINIST PARTY, IN A MANUAL OF THE PARTY'S
OFFICIAL SEX GUIDELINES

"I tell the women that the face is my experience
and the hands are my soul—anything to get those panties down."

CHARLES BUKOWSKI, POET

"You are suggesting I have some sort
of romantic attachment. I have no relationship with her, just a passing
acquaintance for two nights."

MICK JAGGER, WHEN ASKED ABOUT MARGARET TRUDEAU

"I just tell him who my dad is, that that sort of takes care of it."

DEBBY BOONE, PAT BOONE'S DAUGHTER, WHEN ASKED WHAT SHE DOES
WHEN A MAN TRIES TO PICK HER UP

"Why the hell should I get a wife when the man next door's got one?"

FURRY LEWIS, EIGHTY-SEVEN-YEAR-OLD BLUES ARTIST, WHEN ASKED
WHY HE NEVER MARRIED

"I'm glad to hear
that you have a girlfriend. I'm sure your parents are pleased also."

ED DAVIS, LOS ANGELES POLICE CHIEF, TALKING TO JERRY BROWN
ABOUT LINDA RONSTADT

"In Hollywood, all marriages are happy.
It's trying to live together afterward that causes the problems."

SHELLEY WINTERS

"I keep saying I wish I had as much
in bed as I get in the newspapers. I'd be real busy."

LINDA RONSTADT

"A number of bachelors are very grateful to me this week."

HENRY KISSINGER AFTER HIS MARRIAGE TO NANCY MAGINNES

"It's just handy to fuck your best friend."

JOHN LENNON ON YOKO ONO

"Let's put it this way—he refrains from coming."

BRIAN WILSON'S WIFE, MARILYN, COMMENTING ON REPORTS HE WAS
EXPERIMENTING WITH CELIBACY

"Give me two days alone with him, and of course he'll want to marry me."

MARILYN MONROE, WHEN ASKED IF SHE THOUGHT SHE COULD GET
PRINCE RAINIER TO THE ALTAR

"Whatever happened to the real men
in this world, men like Clark Gable? No one would have carried my
daughter off if there'd been a real man there."

CATHERINE HEARST

JOHN LENNON, YOKO ONO, DICK CAVETT/photos by Chuck Pulin

"America is lacking men with,
if I might use the term, male gonads, who are willing to stand up
and fight for what they believe is right."

ED DAVIS, LOS ANGELES POLICE CHIEF

"I thought if I could do it
as an experiment, then fifteen-year-old boys could do it, and that would
make me very happy."

PATTI SMITH, TALKING ABOUT JERKING OFF TO HER OWN PICTURE

"We are definitely
calling it a success. We have sensation, function, and tests to prove it."

DR. CHARLES PAPPAS, PART OF THE FIRST SURGICAL TEAM TO REIMPLANT
A PENIS AND TESTICLE.

"Hell, man, if someone had said
ah had the biggest dick in America, ah'd be happier
than a dog in heat. . . . Rick told me not to mention their names about
anything again. They must want to get a Billy Graham image or something,
though that will be pretty hard, I figure."

RONNIE HAWKINS ON THE BAND'S REACTION TO AN INTERVIEW IN WHICH HE
SPOKE OF LEVON HELM'S NATURAL ENDOWMENTS

"I had the first real hard-on
of my whole life right on camera, and they had to cut
the filming and make everybody wait until it went down.
I sure as hell knew something was happening, but I wasn't sure what
until later. One of the older guys took me aside and explained."

DENNIS DAY ON HIS YEARS AS A MOUSEKETEER

"I didn't know how babies were made
until I was pregnant with my fourth child five years later."

LORETTA LYNN, WHO MARRIED AT AGE THIRTEEN

"It is nothing more than sex education,
essential and necessary in his growth toward maturity and subsequent
domestic family life."

A SANTA FE JUDGE RULING ON INCEST

"She's a piece of ass.
It bothers me. If she looks at another man, I'll kill her."

JAMES TAYLOR ON WIFE CARLY SIMON'S SEXY IMAGE

"I feel that being attractive sexually
is great, and when I stop attracting people sexually then I'll become
a cook or something."

CARLY SIMON

"I don't think there is sex
in heaven. If people only want to go to heaven for sex, they'd better
have heaven on earth."

BILLY GRAHAM

"There will be sex after death—we just won't be able to feel it."

LILY TOMLIN

"[This is a] sickness of Americans.
They have to have intercourse. Virtue is self-discipline."

REPRESENTATIVE JOHN M. ZWACH IN A 1974 CONGRESSIONAL DEBATE ON ABORTION

"I think people should be free at sex—they should draw the line at goats."

ELTON JOHN

"Well, there are a lot of girls into that;
they dig it, they want to be chained up—and it's a thing that's true
for both sexes."

MICK JAGGER ON THE CONTROVERSIAL BONDAGE POSTER FOR THE
BLACK & BLUE ALBUM

"Whether Queen Elizabeth sleeps with Prince Philip
or not is her affair. I think that if you swing with chickens, that is your
perfect right."

LIBERACE

"Whatever she wants to do. There's
other things she could do. She can get married and raise kids
or something like that. Preferably I would not want my daughters in
there, but not because I think it's wrong."

JOE CONFORTE, ASKED IF HE WOULD ENCOURAGE
HIS DAUGHTERS TO GO INTO HIS BUSINESS

"Police should go after drunk drivers who kill
thousands of people instead of prostitutes who entertain thousands."

DR. JENNIFER JAMES, ANTHROPOLOGIST, ON A NATIONWIDE CAMPAIGN
TO DECRIMINALIZE PROSTITUTION

ELTON JOHN/photo by James Shive

"If a girl wants to screw,
whether she charges or not, it's her business.
The moralists, they say it's immoral. How can anything be immoral if it
hurts no one and gives people pleasure? Morality is a thought, it's
not a fact—it's not a thing you can see."

JOE CONFORTE, BROTHEL OWNER, DEFENDING PROSTITUTION

"I wouldn't know her if she was to fall on top of me."

REPRESENTATIVE JOHN DINGELL, IN 1976, CLAIMING NO MEMORY OF THE
CALL GIRL ALLEGEDLY PROCURED FOR HIM

"Murder and prostitution excite me.
Let's face it. The desire of all photographers is to
photograph murder with a knife instead of a gun, preferably. That's
what makes covering wars so exciting."

DENNIS HOPPER

"Someone once said to me that nothing is real
in L.A. unless it's genuinely fake, and I find it amusing
that America props up its marriages and sex lives through a pair of
crotchless knickers. It's like marriage guidance in plain brown wrappers."

BOOMTOWN RATS' BOB GELDOF AT FREDERICK'S OF HOLLYWOOD

"I can't understand why more people aren't
bisexual. It would double your chances for a date on Saturday night."

WOODY ALLEN, ADMITTED HETEROSEXUAL

"Do you know why God hates homosexuality?
Because the male homosexual eats another man's sperm. Sperm is the
most concentrated form of blood. The homosexual is eating life."

ANITA BRYANT

"I guess they're entitled to remain as sick as they like as long as they like."

SENATOR S.I. HAYAKAWA IN 1977 ON HOMOSEXUALS

"The right wing needs these witch hunts. . . .
They believe fags are going to break into the toilets and
piss on lovely virgins."

AUTHOR GORE VIDAL

"Now I don't think you can necessarily
equate Farm Workers with people with unusual sexual preferences, but
I suppose you could call them united fruit workers."

ED DAVIS, LOS ANGELES POLICE CHIEF

"They ruined a perfectly good theater
by filling it with faggots in boxing shorts waving champagne bottles
in front of your face."

KEITH RICHARDS' ASSESSMENT OF STUDIO 54

"If homosexuality were the normal way,
God would have made Adam and Bruce."

ANITA BRYANT

"Children cannot act like adults,
women can't be bricklayers and plumbers,
and homosexuals have no place in the police department."

GILBERT LINDSAY, LOS ANGELES CITY COUNCIL MEMBER

"At least it's a fruit pie."

ANITA BRYANT, AFTER A BANANA-CREAM PIE WAS THROWN IN HER FACE
BY A GAY

"This place is more than my living now—
it's my mission. I've led a whole sexual revolution here, and
I'm ready to expand beyond these walls. To be used by the people.
Yes! I'm speaking of politics."

STEPHEN OSTROW, CONTINENTAL BATHS OWNER

"Decadence rules—it's so lovely,
so unlimited, so natural. If Jesus Christ came back again, and took me for
a beer, I'd never change. I mean, he was one helluva strange boy himself."

WAYNE COUNTY, TRANSVESTITE GLITTER-ROCKER

"We have to allow for marginal people—
for the unusual, the deviant. I'm all for deviants."

WRITER-CRITIC SUSAN SONTAG

"I don't think about deep things—
if you can't take a bite of it, it doesn't exist."

TED NUGENT

"In California, everyone goes to a therapist,
is a therapist, or is a therapist going to a therapist."

TRUMAN CAPOTE

"I don't understand a word of it, but
if it makes Rum Dum happy, it's okay with me."

GEORGE ALPERT, BABA RAM DAS' FATHER, ON HIS SON'S PHILOSOPHY

"In the Far East the master is considered
a living Buddha, but in Minneapolis they wonder why he
doesn't have a job."

ROBERT M. PIRSIG, AUTHOR OF *ZEN AND THE ART OF MOTORCYCLE MAINTENANCE*

"Buddha was a good guy, but history is full of good guys."

CLIFF RICHARD, BORN-AGAIN RECORDING ARTIST

"I always knew the Buddha could
come in all forms, but I never figured him for a janitor."

BABA RAM DAS, VISITING A RELIGIOUS COMMUNE THAT SUPPORTS ITSELF
IN PART BY RUNNING A MAINTENANCE AND CUSTODIAL COMPANY

"Visiting the holy men is just like visiting
the Hearsts—you're both obsessed with the servant problem."

JOURNALIST PAUL KRASSNER, WHILE WITH
BABA RAM DAS AND BHAGWAN DAS

"I don't wanna take no year's sabbatical
and go see some guru in the Himalayas to learn the secret of life. I don't
think there's too many secrets to life, really."

CHARLIE DANIELS

"The world has shown me what it has
to offer. . . . It's a nice place to visit, but I wouldn't want to live there."

ARLO GUTHRIE

"Transcendental meditation is evil,
because when you are meditating, it opens space within you for the
devil to enter."

BILLY GRAHAM

"I've never been a fan of
personality-conflict burgers and identity-crisis omelets with patchouli
oil. I function very well on a diet that consists of Chicken Catastrophe
and Eggs Overwhelming and a tall, cool Janitor-in-a-Drum. I like to
walk out of a restaurant with enough gas to open
a Mobil station."

TOM WAITS

"Anything that is in excess is bad;
you can have an excess of government, and excess is bad. Except maybe in
religion, I don't think you can have an excess of religion."

LEO THORSNESS, FORMER POW, RUNNING FOR THE U.S. SENATE
AGAINST GEORGE McGOVERN

"As long as you don't talk about politics or
religion, you can get along with a lot of people."

MICHAEL DOUGLAS

"Brothers and sisters, where are you at?
You can cop out on the whole scene . . . you can bad-mouth Jesus . . . or
you can let him turn you on to heavy vibes of forever joy. Dig it!
Like, the decision is yours."

THE NEW YORK BIBLE SOCIETY, 1973

"I am one of those cliff-hanging Catholics.
I don't believe in God, but I do believe that Mary was his mother."

ACTOR MARTIN SHEEN

"The nuns turn you into a wimp,
totally dominated by your mother or your wife. Or you can become so
hard-core that you can survive, like us."

JIMMY ZERO OF THE DEAD BOYS

"No, I'm not. I've had myself
shortened by two feet, [had] bone grafts for ten years on my nose, and I
had my eyes pushed together for that beady-eyed look. I had to do it to
be a success in show biz."

MEL BROOKS, WHEN ASKED IF HE WERE JEWISH

"I think the Pope came [to the U.S.]
on the holiest day of the year—Yom Kippur."

RON ALEXENBURG, INFINITY RECORDS' PRESIDENT

"I gave up rock & roll for the Rock of Ages. If God can save me, an old homosexual, he can save anybody."

LITTLE RICHARD PENNIMAN, PREACHING AGAINST THE MUSIC HE HELPED PIONEER

"A lot of people would love to go to the Holy Land, but there's two reasons they don't go—the time and the money! They'll be able to come here for maybe five or ten bucks a day, and see more of the Holy Land as it really was like 2000 years ago than if they spent a hundred times that to go over there."

BILL CAYWOOD ON A PROPOSAL TO BUILD HOLYLAND, USA, A "DISNEY-TYPE" THEME PARK

"We are bringing the Bible to life. We are presenting Christ, presenting Jonah, presenting the characters of the Bible—bringing them to life, and letting them be as well-known as . . . Mickey Mouse or Donald Duck!"

BILL CAYWOOD OF HOLYLAND, USA

"I don't think there's any other religion in the whole United States that can say it's got 100,000 ordained ministers. If ya look at it that way, we're as big as any Christian religion."

REVEREND KIRBY J. HENSLEY, PRESIDENT OF UNIVERSAL LIFE CHURCH

"Different strokes for different folks. I sort of consider myself a contemporary gadfly. The Universal Life Church gives me a chance to dip my tail into the ointment and stir up some shit."

REVEREND KIRBY J. HENSLEY, PRESIDENT OF UNIVERSAL LIFE CHURCH

"They're an honest collector's item.
Certainly there won't be any more albums by this group."

TRAVIS T. HIPP OF KFAT-FM IN GILROY, CALIFORNIA, EXPLAINING WHY THE
STATION BOUGHT 300 LPs BY THE PEOPLE'S TEMPLE CHOIR

"I suppose you must be talking about Jonestown
or some asshole, scum-of-the-earth, goat-tit worm debris like that. That
shit just ricochets off my mind. They are floundering scab tissue
with no rights whatsoever."

TED NUGENT, WHEN ASKED ABOUT MESSIAH FOLLOWERS

"If you tell me hippies and yippies are
going to be able to do the job of helping America, I'll tell you this: they
can't run a bus; they can't serve in a government office; they can't
run a lathe in a factory. All they can do is lay down in the park
and sleep or kick policemen."

SPIRO AGNEW

"We were on a plane once with Colonel Sanders . . .
and Dewey, the drummer, went into the first-class section and started
talking to Colonel Sanders. He said, 'Tell me, Colonel, do you
like hippies?' And he says, 'Well, dey eats chicken, don't dey?' "

COUNTRY JOE McDONALD

"A hippie is another word for a goat tick. If a guy's got flies
buzzing around his head and a joint in his mouth, I think he's a sap."

TED NUGENT

"The parody of the space cadet, in my mind,
is the guy who believes that if you really eat enough organic honey,
everything's going to work out all right."

DAVID HARRIS

"Jerry [Rubin] and Abbie [Hoffman]
couldn't organize a luncheon, much less a revolution."

SAUL ALINSKY, POVERTY FIGHTER

"I guess I don't like someone pissing on my head and calling it rain."

GEORGE YUDICH, AIR FORCE VETERAN, RADICALIZED BY POLICE BEHAVIOR
AT THE 1968 CHICAGO CONVENTION

"They could mark the beginning of an era
of disorderliness, complacency, and apathy—a lack of pride in individual
and country, which could sap our vitality. This could be, I said. My
guess is that it will not."

WILLIAM WESTMORELAND, RETIRED HEAD OF THE JOINT CHIEFS OF STAFF,
ON LONGHAIRED YOUTH

"It is the most exciting thing
since my tenth birthday when I rode a roller coaster for the first time."

S.I. HAYAKAWA, REFERRING TO EVENTS ON THE SAN FRANCISCO STATE
CAMPUS, WHEN NINE PERSONS WERE VICTIMS OF VIOLENCE

"They are the worst type of people we harbor
in America . . . worse than brown shirts and the Communist element."

OHIO GOVERNOR JAMES RHODES, REFLECTING IN 1975 ABOUT
THE KENT STATE DEMONSTRATORS

"We can't send enough soldiers and policemen
onto these campuses, and if we have to shut the institutions of higher
learning down and put that money into primary education, maybe
that's what the State of California and America had better
start thinking about doing."

ED DAVIS, LOS ANGELES POLICE CHIEF, ON STUDENT UNREST

"We can afford to separate them [protesters]
from our society with no more regret than we should feel over
discarding rotten apples from a barrel."

SPIRO AGNEW

"Any student at any university in the United States
who has an idea on how to bridge the gap between students and
government should write it down and send it to the White House."

TRICIA NIXON

"In this battle, Timothy, we need every mind
and every soul, but oh my doctor, we don't need one more nut with a gun."

AUTHOR KEN KESEY IN AN OPEN LETTER TO TIMOTHY LEARY

"Call it paranoia. But paranoia for peace isn't that bad."

RICHARD NIXON ON HIS REACTION TO DISSIDENTS

"We met the enemy, and he was us."

GENERAL WILLIAM WESTMORELAND ON VIETNAM

"The B-52 has been an effective war machine. It's killed a lot of people."

REPRESENTATIVE BILL YOUNG, SPEAKING ON THE FLOOR OF THE HOUSE OF
REPRESENTATIVES IN 1975

"The B-52 has been an effective war machine
which unfortunately has killed a lot of people."

REPRESENTATIVE BILL YOUNG AFTER HIS REMARKS WERE "SANITIZED"
FOR PUBLICATION IN THE *CONGRESSIONAL RECORD*

"If worse comes to worse and he must faint,
a soldier should fall to the ground under control. To do so, he must
turn his body approximately forty-five degrees, squat down, roll to the
left, and retain control of his weapon. . . . Every incident of fainting will
be investigated by the section commander. We must ensure that
soldiers who have not complied with the above instructions
be charged."

DETAILS OF A MEMO TO CANADIAN TROOPS, DISCLOSED IN 1976 BY
JOHN REYNOLDS, MEMBER OF PARLIAMENT

"We made the decision not to start up any war feeling
in the country because we thought it was too dangerous for the people
of a democracy to get too angry in a nuclear world. We were asking
our people who were carrying on the battle to do something
in hot blood that we were doing back here in cold blood."

DEAN RUSK, FORMER U.S. SECRETARY OF STATE, 1978

"It's getting pretty desperate when you
have to shoot somebody with a bullet just to say hello."

CAPTAIN BEEFHEART ON THE VIETNAM WAR

RONALD REAGAN/photo by Movie Star News

"The only thing we were guilty of was premature morality."

STANLEY J. PIETLOCK, DRAFT EVADER

☙

"Let's pave it."

RONALD REAGAN ON VIETNAM

☙

"The marines are a can-do outfit, one of the
greatest can-do outfits since the Los Angeles Police Department."

ED DAVIS, LOS ANGELES POLICE CHIEF

☙

" 'Peace' is when nobody's shooting.
A 'just peace' is when our side gets what it wants."

CARTOONIST BILL MAULDIN

☙

"The war's not over. The war
is between those who catch hell and those who give it out. Just 'cause
it's not on TV don't mean they stopped giving it out."

VIETNAM VETERAN RON KOVIC

☙

"Vietnamese kids are toilet trained
by the time they can sit, and they don't seem to have problems."

JANE FONDA, COMPARING CULTURES

"My sister says power to the people. I say to hell with the
people. . . . This whole mess we're in has been brought about by people."

PETER FONDA

"Everybody will disagree with me,
but I believe in blowing the hell out of them."

SENATOR JAMES EASTLAND ON THE NORTH KOREAN CAPTURE OF THE *MAYAGUEZ*

"We were sitting in the bow of the yacht.
I'm an old navy man; the bow is the rear end, isn't it?"

RICHARD NIXON DURING HIS INTERVIEW WITH DAVID FROST

"People seem less interested in survival, more in the
return of the frontier or maybe a sudden desert island. Fat chance."

STEWART BRAND, *WHOLE EARTH CATALOG* FOUNDER AND EDITOR

"Now we're in a period . . . where the fundamental
passion of the young is to snigger at the worn-out aspirations of the
middle-aged. . . . Now we're in some sort of post-fascisto, apathetic
hippie beatdom. Everybody feels that somehow there is
shit in the nectar."

NORMAN MAILER

"The student now goes to college to proclaim
rather than to learn. . . . A spirit of national masochism prevails,
encouraged by an effete corps of impudent snobs who
characterize themselves as intellectuals."

SPIRO AGNEW ON HIGHER EDUCATION

"Law and order is like patriotism—anyone who
comes on strong about patriotism has got something to hide; it never fails.
They always turn out to be a crook or an asshole or a
traitor or something."

CARTOONIST BILL MAULDIN

"I've said it before and I'll say it again. I'm gonna
live in the world I want to live in. You people who run things ain't got
nothin' to be proud of; you've left things in one hell of a mess."

SONNY BARGER, UNREPENTANT HELL'S ANGELS PRESIDENT

"I hope this verdict will be a lesson
to the young people of this country—that you just can't go into a
person's house and butcher them up."

JUROR MARIE MESMER, IN 1971, DISCUSSING THE VERDICT FOR THE DEATH
PENALTY GIVEN CHARLES MANSON AND HIS FOLLOWERS, PATRICIA
KRENWINKEL, SUSAN ATKINS, AND LESLIE VAN HOUTEN

"We should distinguish between the two kinds of violence.
If someone is violent toward those who seek freedom, that's bad. But if
those who seek freedom use violence to achieve it, that's good."

FILMMAKER MICHELANGELO ANTONIONI

"I have a definitional problem with the word
violence. I don't know what the word *violence* means."

CIA DIRECTOR WILLIAM COLBY IN 1975

"I hate violence. If some security geezer hurts a kid, I'll bust him."

ALEX HARVEY, BRITISH ROCK STAR

"Nothing is illegal if a hundred businessmen
decide to do it, and that's true anywhere in the world."

ANDREW YOUNG

🌱

"They thought it was a compliment
to be called 'a hell of a businessman.' Well, that means you're a weasel.
Hitler was a hell of a businessman."

B. KLIBAN, CARTOONIST, ON AD AGENCIES

🌱

"I like my goodies too. . . .
Maybe what I did was wrong. If it was, I'm sorry."

KEN MOSS, ASKED ABOUT FALSE ADVERTISING AND THE THOUSANDS OF DOLLARS
IN UNPAID REFUNDS OWED TO CUSTOMERS FOR HIS BOGUS
AIR TRAVEL CLUB, FREELANDIA

🌱

"It is the inalienable right of every shoplifter
to do his or her thing if he or she can get away with it. This is a tribute
to the store's quality merchandise."

CASABLANCA RECORDS' CHUCK ASHMAN, REACTING TO A DEPARTMENT STORE
THAT WAS PILFERED DURING A COMMODORES AUTOGRAPH PARTY

🌱

"I didn't need money, I needed freedom, and . . . I got my freedom,
so they served their purpose very well, and if anybody thinks
otherwise, then they're capitalistic."

RUBIN "HURRICANE" CARTER, RESPONDING TO CRITICISM ON EXPENSES
FOR "NIGHT OF THE HURRICANE" CONCERTS

🌱

"I never said I was tough on crime."

EVELLE YOUNGER, CALIFORNIA ATTORNEY GENERAL, 1978, REPLYING TO
WELL-DOCUMENTED CHARGES THAT HE WAS FRIENDLY TO MOB INTERESTS

"Well, I never heard of you either."

TOM WAITS, REPLYING TO A LOS ANGELES COP WHO PULLED HIM OVER
AND FAILED TO RECOGNIZE THE SINGER

"I hope that one gets to court.
I really wanna find out what an emotionally disturbed cow is into."

JOHN JAYMES ON BEING SUED BY AN ALTAMONT RANCHER FOR DAMAGES,
INCLUDING "EMOTIONALLY DISTURBING" HIS COWS

"One person threw a rock,
and then, like monkeys in a zoo, others started throwing rocks."

BILL PARKER, LOS ANGELES POLICE CHIEF, ON THE WATTS RIOTS

"Sin began with Adam. If you
turn the lights out, folks will steal. They'll do that in Switzerland, too."

ANDREW YOUNG ON LOOTING DURING A BLACKOUT IN NEW YORK CITY

"You can't shoot people when your life's not in danger.
If a guy's blown away in an armed robbery, tough twinkies."

LAWYER JOHN CARTER

"I'm not mean—never have been mean—but I
can tell you this: I'd rather be tried for killing some sorry
son-of-a-bitch than have him tried for killing me."

A.Y. ALLEE, TEXAS RANGERS CAPTAIN, DISMISSING CRITICISM OF HIS TACTICS

"Would Chairman Mao steal socks?"

LOS ANGELES COP, AFTER A SYMBIONESE LIBERATION ARMY SHOPLIFTING INCIDENT

🌿

"Garroting is a more humane form
of executing a criminal than any other way. It is quick, clean, and there
is no blood."

PASCUAL VILLAR ALBERTO, SPANISH AMBASSADOR, ON A RECENT EXECUTION OF
TWO SPANISH MURDERERS BY GARROTING, A FORM OF STRANGULATION
USING AN IRON COLLAR TIGHTENED AROUND THE NECK BY A SCREW

🌿

"I'm in favor of the death penalty. . . . I think it saves lives."

NANCY REAGAN, WIFE OF RONALD REAGAN

🌿

"The Supreme Court's decision to ban the death penalty
is an absurdity. It violates any plain simple country boy's interpretation
of the Constitution. The death penalty is the strongest link in our system
of justice. Without it, policemen will be like they're castrated."

ED DAVIS, LOS ANGELES POLICE CHIEF

🌿

"I hope we'll see some electrocutions
in this state. If it's not a deterrent, at least it'll
get some folks off the public's back, permanently."

GEORGE WALLACE

🌿

"If they can't find someone to pull the switch, I'll do it."

FRANK RIZZO, PHILADELPHIA MAYOR, ON CAPITAL PUNISHMENT

"We don't use the gun to slow a person down, we shoot to kill him."

CLEVELAND FUESSENICH, CONNECTICUT STATE POLICE COMMISSIONER, ON HIS
DEPARTMENT'S SWITCH TO HOLLOW-POINT BULLETS, BANNED BY
THE GENEVA CONVENTION

"I would recommend we have a portable courtroom
on a big bus and a portable gallows, and after we get the death penalty
put back in, we conduct a rapid trial for a hijacker, and we hang him
with due process of law out there at the airport."

ED DAVIS, LOS ANGELES POLICE CHIEF

"You have to go to a certain extent on hearsay.
You're not always meticulous in observing the rules of evidence when
considering a presentencing report."

JUDGE DON KENNEDY OF GREENFIELD, MISSOURI, AFTER DENYING PROBATION
IN A POT CASE

"This trial has sex, glamour, Andy Williams . . . and besides,
everybody's just come off the most boring presidential campaign in history."

REPORTER COVERING CLAUDINE LONGET'S TRIAL FOR MANSLAUGHTER

"Their sexual juices really start to flow
at fourteen, fifteen, and sixteen. It doesn't take much to provoke a guy.
Whether you like it or not, a woman's a sex object, and they're the ones
who turn the man on, generally."

JUDGE ARCHIE SIMONSON OF MADISON, WISCONSIN, REFUSING TO CONFINE
A FIFTEEN-YEAR-OLD BOY FOR RAPING A SIXTEEN-YEAR-OLD GIRL

"You can't blame a man for trying."

WALTER PICKET, CONNECTICUT JUDGE, AFTER DISMISSING A
RAPE CONSPIRACY CHARGE

❦

"Even in open court we have . . . women appearing
without bras, nipples fully exposed, and they think it is smart, and they
sit there on the witness stand with their dresses up over the
cheeks of their butts."

JUDGE SIMONSON, VIEWING RAPE AS A "NORMAL REACTION"
TO A PERMISSIVE SEXUAL ATMOSPHERE IN MADISON, WISCONSIN

❦

"Good people, fine people
from fine backgrounds, just don't kill people in cold blood."

DOUG SCHMIDT, DEFENSE ATTORNEY FOR EX-CITY OFFICIAL DAN WHITE,
WHO KILLED SAN FRANCISCO MAYOR GEORGE MOSCONE
AND GAY CITY SUPERVISOR HARVEY MILK

❦

"Society doesn't have anything
to do with it, only those twelve people in the jury box."

DEFENSE ATTORNEY DOUG SCHMIDT, WHEN ASKED IF SOCIETY WOULD FEEL
JUSTICE HAD BEEN SERVED IN THE MURDER TRIAL OF DAN WHITE

❦

"I want you to know we're here today
because we care. I don't know what we care about, but we care."

JOHNNY CASH, PLAYING AT LEAVENWORTH PRISON

❦

"What I like about this is that it's
the first outdoor concert I've ever done with no security problems."

BILL GRAHAM, PUTTING ON A SHOW AT SOLEDAD PRISON

"I carried a .38. I would rehearse the holdups
with it in front of a mirror, trying different ways to see which seemed
the most treacherous. You heard about that nervous armed robber who
said, 'Okay, mothersticker, this is a fuckup'? Well, that was me.
I still don't know whether I'd've used it."

JUDEE SILL, SINGER/SONGWRITER

"Her room was probably better in prison."

CATHERINE HEARST ON HER DAUGHTER'S RETURN HOME

"I'm terrified by the thought of being haunted
by all the animals I've eaten in my lifetime. Can you imagine it? All those
cows, sheeps, and chickens clucking around in white sheets?"

LOL CREME OF 10cc, IN 1975

"I don't pay to have my dirty work done for me.
I do it myself. Animals were put here for human beings to use. Anyone
who says that man is not a predator is a sap."

TED NUGENT

"Pretty soon we won't be able to get guns
to go duck hunting. Then there will be an overpopulation of ducks."

REPRESENTATIVE RON DELLUMS, ARGUING AGAINST GUN CONTROL, IN 1975

"How perfect an existence for fish
to float in the water and swim and let food float by and they get it.
How far out it is to be a bird and fly around the trees. I am what I've
always wanted to be and that is the truth."

JOHN DENVER

"I've always liked reptiles. I used to
see the universe as a mammoth peristaltic snake,
and I used to see all the people and objects and landscapes as little
pictures on the facets of their scales. I think peristaltic motion
is the basic life movement. It's swallowing, digestion,
and the rhythms of sexual intercourse."

JIM MORRISON

"Stupidity is the devil. Look in the eye of
a chicken and you'll know. It's the most horrifying, cannibalistic,
and nightmarish creature in this world."

FILMMAKER WERNER HERZOG

"I think I'd be happy just living with
a marine biologist in the middle of the ocean . . . studying fishes."

LINDA RONSTADT

"You can make believe you're chickens,
you can make believe you're Martians, you can make believe you're
androgynous, but you can't make believe you're friends."

DENNIS LOCORRIERE OF DR. HOOK ON THE BAND'S CAMARADERIE
FORGED BY DIFFICULT EARLY DAYS

"My friends won't come over. It's a hovel.
My landlord is about ninety. He's always coming over
and asking me if I live here. And my neighbor up front is a throwback
to the Fifties, an old harlot. . . . I wake up to that. But I need
a place that's cluttered so I can see the chaos. It's like a
visual thesaurus."

TOM WAITS ON HIS LIFE-STYLE

"It's not really explainable, but you feel pleasant inside a dome. It's like cocaine. It's mildly euphoric—but you can't define it."

PAUL KANTNER

"We all lead more pedestrian lives
than we think we do. The boiling of an egg is sometimes more important
than the boiling of a love affair in the end."

LILLIAN HELLMAN

"It's really a hard thing to get the bacon right."

TRICIA NIXON COX ON COOKING

"There are times to think
and times not to think. Fuck trouble, baby. . . . But I've made some
mistakes I wish I hadn't."

LEE MARVIN ON HIS ROUGH-AND-TUMBLE LIFE-STYLE

"The best and the worst thing
that happened to me in 1976 was that I lived through it."

ACTRESS LOUISE LASSER

"I think that cynicism is a positive value. . . .
The more people that I can encourage to be cynical, the
better job I think I have done."

FRANK ZAPPA

"Life is not for everybody."

MICHAEL O'DONOGHUE

"My dear, what is time?
You're talking to the person who brought you the sixties."

TIMOTHY LEARY, RESPONDING TO A REMINDER HE HAD PREDICTED
THE COLLAPSE OF AMERICA IN 1980

"Being powerful is like being a lady.
If you have to tell people you are, you ain't."

JESSE CARR, HEAD OF ANCHORAGE TEAMSTERS' UNION, 1976

"One of my favorite philosophical tenets
is that people will agree with you only if they already agree with you.
You do not change people's minds."

FRANK ZAPPA

"The truth as you want to know it?
Oh, no, dear boy. No, I'm afraid you couldn't afford me."

KEITH MOON, ASKED BY A CAMERAMAN TO TELL THE TRUTH FOR ONCE

"Most of my biggest problems now
are what color scheme to use on my next string of beads."

JANIS JOPLIN

"It's made out of fucking creosote. . . .
It made me smell like someone just did a pavement job on my head."

BALD RON NAGLE ON HIS FATHER'S HAIR RESTORER

🌱

"What's the point of being famous if you're still lame?"

RANDY NEWMAN ON FEELING CLUMSY IN SOCIAL SITUATIONS

🌱

"That's . . . a very good way to keep
from crying: take five deep breaths. It always works."

JULIE NIXON EISENHOWER

🌱

"I've probably had more of a chance
to make an asshole out of myself than most people,
and I realize that. But then not everybody gets a chance to live out
their nightmares for the vicarious pleasures of the public."

LOU REED

🌱

"I wish I was with my friends tonight,
destroying my hometown. . . . You know, I stole
seventeen cars in high school. I derailed a train with a rock.
Me and my friends blew up all the thermostats in school with
plastic explosives. We stole bowling balls and threw them into buildings
from our cars at ninety miles an hour. We got rancid whipped cream
from garbage cans at the Reddi-Whip factory and put it in fire
extinguishers and sprayed it on people. It was the
best time of my life."

MARK MENDOZA OF THE DICTATORS

"That's the old American way—if you got a good thing, then overdo it."

PHIL WALDEN, PRESIDENT OF CAPRICORN RECORDS, 1976

"Neil Armstrong was the first man
to walk on the moon. I am the first man to piss his pants on the moon."

BUZZ ALDRIN

"It's ridiculous to think that we're evacuating
an area of 100,000 square kilometers. We only evacuate the launch area
and a small impact area when we have tests. We put the Africans
on a truck and make a big festival five kilometers away."

FRANK WUKASCH, EXECUTIVE OF OTRAG, THE WEST GERMAN COMPANY OF SPACE
ENTREPRENEURS, TALKING ABOUT THEIR ROCKET LAUNCHES IN ZAIRE

"NASA wanted to develop a space pen
for the astronauts. They wanted a pen that would
write upside down, that would write in a vacuum. They spent
more than half a million dollars to develop a pen that would do those
things. And they could have used a normal pencil."

FRANK WUKASCH, EXECUTIVE OF OTRAG, A WEST GERMAN COMPANY
OF SPACE ENTREPRENEURS

"As one of that generation of Americans
who had the pants scared off them by that Orson Welles
invasion from Mars broadcast in 1938, I'm glad to hear that there isn't
any life on Mars."

LYNDON JOHNSON, AFTER MARINER IV PHOTOS INDICATED
MARS IS A DEAD PLANET

DAVID BOWIE/photo by Chuck Pulin

"There's a difference between a contradiction
and a paradox. A contradiction stops things. A paradox makes them grow."

STEWART BRAND, *WHOLE EARTH CATALOG* CREATOR, ASKED IF HIS SPACE
BOOSTERISM DIDN'T CONTRADICT HIS PAST CONCERNS

"I already consider myself
responsible for a whole new school of pretension."

DAVID BOWIE

"When I hear the word *culture,* I reach for my revolver."

HERMANN GOERING

"When I see a long word I don't know, I take it out."

LARRY FLYNT, PUBLISHER OF *HUSTLER*

"Sometimes I like to indulge in them myself."

JULIE NIXON EISENHOWER, CONFESSING HER WEAKNESS FOR EXPLETIVES DELETED

"If the reason they pulled the album is because of language,
fuck them. . . . It's interesting that they waited for the record to sell
3 million copies before they decided to pull it."

STEVE MARTIN, AFTER K-MART REMOVED *A WILD AND CRAZY GUY*
FROM ITS STORES

"If this doesn't put the cunt back in country, I don't know what will."

CARLENE CARTER, INTRODUCING "SWAP-MEAT RAG," A SONG
ABOUT HUSBAND SWAPPING

"So what's wrong with cheap,
dirty jokes? Fuck you. I never said I was tasteful. I'm *not* tasteful."

LOU REED, RESPONDING TO CRITICISM OF ETHNIC SLURS IN HIS SONGS

"I apologize, motherfucker, that
I am a human being. I fucking apologize.
Emotional—you're fucking right. . . . You're
full of shit, and I have more fucking balls than you'll
ever see. You want to challenge me about emotions, you slimy
little man. Fuck you. Fuck you. Don't get peaceful
with me. Don't you touch me."

BILL GRAHAM'S REPLY IN 1969 TO STEVE GASKIN, WHO ASSERTED
GRAHAM CHOSE MONEY OVER LOVE

"Goddam it, Nelson, son of a bitch!
I've always wanted to be a Great American,
and now you're going to fuck it up! You suck one cock
and they call you a cocksucker!"

ATTORNEY GENERAL RICHARD KLEINDIENST, REPLYING TO JACK NELSON
OF THE *LOS ANGELES TIMES* ABOUT THE "GREAT AMERICAN" AWARD
HE'D JUST RECEIVED IN 1973 FROM A ONE-MAN
COMIC BOOK HOUSE

"Rock journalism is people who
can't write interviewing people who can't talk
for people who can't read."

FRANK ZAPPA

"I always wanted to be some kind
of writer or newspaper reporter. But after college . . . I did other things."

JACQUELINE KENNEDY ONASSIS

"Last May I wanted to interview Mick Jagger.
I'd thought about a journalism career until I found out just what it was like."

CARLY SIMON

"To penetrate the cacophony
of seditious drivel emanating from the
best-publicized clowns in our society and their fans
in the Fourth Estate . . . we need a cry of alarm, not a whisper."

SPIRO AGNEW

"It's amazing what he has done
to the media . . . helping it to reform itself.
I'm a close watcher of newspapers and TV. I think they've
taken a second look. You can't underestimate the power of fear."

TRICIA NIXON COX, ADMIRING SPIRO AGNEW

"No New Yorker should take Rupert Murdoch's
New York Post seriously any longer. It makes *Hustler* magazine
look like the *Harvard* [Law] *Review*."

ABE BEAME, NEW YORK MAYOR, 1977

"I can't even count on one hand
five people of any importance in the media who aren't Jewish. I can't."

TRUMAN CAPOTE

TRUMAN CAPOTE/photo by UPI

"Why is it that your newspaper
insists on running photographs that make my nose
look two or three inches longer than it really is? I didn't
know that your paper was anti-Semitic."

CHICAGO SEVEN JUDGE JULIUS HOFFMAN, SPEAKING TO
BOB GREENE OF THE *CHICAGO SUN-TIMES*

🦢

"This whole thing has become journalism by checkbook and court order."

RICHARD SPRATLING OF KUTV IN UTAH, DISCUSSING GARY GILMORE AND THE MEDIA

🦢

"I would be better off if I had
leaped the counter and choked the judge. I would be able to get a pardon."

JOURNALIST BILL FARR, JAILED INDEFINITELY IN 1973 FOR NOT
REVEALING HIS SOURCES

🦢

"Trying to discuss this kind of communications
reform at the Capitol is like trying to initiate members of Congress
in the ways of Jupiter and Mars."

RALPH NADER ON MEDIA REFORM EFFORTS

🦢

"Unless you and I fornicate
in front of everybody, people aren't going to think we get along."

BARBARA WALTERS TO CO-ANCHOR HARRY REASONER ON THE
ABC EVENING NEWS

🦢

"This country places a tremendous priority
on being successful, but there is a tremendous lack of people who are
good at what they do."

PAUL SIMON

"There is something odd going on
in this century that we've come to the point
where art, poetry, the novel, . . . almost every form of
advanced and dedicated art have begun to move away from the old
meat and potatoes of art. It's as if the ball of culture in which we wrap
ourselves is beginning to roll off the table."

NORMAN MAILER IN 1973

"Having no talent is no longer enough."

AUTHOR GORE VIDAL

"I've decided that I'm completely corrupt.
My whole act, my economic success, is wholly dependent
upon the existence of segregation, violence, crime, and the other odious
counterparts. If a messiah should return and gamma-ray all the pestilence
and leave the world pure, I would be standing in the breadline. The only
thing that saves my sanity is that I would be standing directly in back
of Jonas Salk and J. Edgar Hoover."

LENNY BRUCE

"What sort of a profession is it
for a grown man to sit around drawing pictures?"

CARTOONIST B. KLIBAN

"The only problem with drawing Nixon
is restraint. Your tendency is to let your feelings come out.
He's such a loathsome son of a bitch, and he looks so loathsome."

CARTOONIST BILL MAULDIN

"If the Stones' lyrics made sense, they wouldn't be any good."
TRUMAN CAPOTE

"I take the Archie tradition of teen-age
American kids, but then it turns into—well, it turns into something else."
R. CRUMB OF ZAP COMIX

"The whole world is a scab. The point is to pick it constructively."
PHOTOGRAPHER PETER BEARD

"If this is art, then eggs are acorns."
RAY MILLER, BRITISH JOURNALIST, ON AN EXHIBIT OF JOHN LENNON'S
CONTROVERSIAL LITHOGRAPHS

"I don't think it is bad taste to be naked; otherwise, every
artist for the last 2000 years would be on trial for nakedness."
JOHN LENNON ON HIS NUDE ALBUM COVER PHOTO

"The only way anybody'd get me to work
was to make the hours from one to two with an hour off for lunch."
POOL HUSTLER MINNESOTA FATS, WHO SAYS HE'S NEVER WORKED A DAY IN HIS LIFE

"I look at comedy with, not a jaundiced eye, but rather a cancerous eye."
MICHAEL O'DONOGHUE

"You can na-noo your heart out. . . . So I try
to work on several levels at once, to slip in tiny innuendos.
It's a game I play with the censors called 'Getting Shit through the
Radar.' Yiddish is good, because the censor is Spanish.
She knows what putz means, though."

ROBIN WILLIAMS

"My way of joking is to tell the truth. That's the funniest joke in the world."

MUHAMMAD ALI

"I never hung out with the other Vegas comedians
anyway. I never went over to Don Adams' house for dinner. I never
bought an alpaca sweater, and I never learned to play golf."

GEORGE CARLIN ON NOT MAKING IT IN LAS VEGAS

"My songs only exist in the essence of silence."

DONOVAN

"Most artists are insecure, I suppose. Insecure overachievers."

LINDSEY BUCKINGHAM OF FLEETWOOD MAC

"Translations are like women.
When they are pretty, chances are they won't be very faithful."

STEVEN SEYMOUR, INTERPRETER WHOSE MISINTERPRETATIONS EMBARRASSED
PRESIDENT CARTER IN POLAND, 1978

"You can't go on doing that thing for years. I mean,
just imagine having to sing 'Satisfaction' when you're forty-five."

MARIANNE FAITHFULL ON SINGING CAREERS

"It's a bit like, I suppose, being married and
having an affair on the side. The affair is always more exciting."

TRUMAN CAPOTE, WHOSE WORK ON *ANSWERED PRAYERS* WAS DELAYED
BY A SECOND BOOK

"I think Shakespeare is shit!
'Thee' and 'thou'; the guy sounds like a faggot."

GENE SIMMONS OF KISS

"Jack Kerouac—that isn't writing, it's typing."

TRUMAN CAPOTE

"All a writer has to do to get a woman
is to say he's a writer. It's an aphrodisiac."

SAUL BELLOW IN 1976

"Having the world love you is not gratifying.
They all applaud, but none of them will come home with you and look at
your back someplace to see if you have a pimple."

GILDA RADNER

"Writing is the toughest thing I've ever done."

RICHARD NIXON

"Finishing a book is just like you took a child out in the yard
and shot it."

TRUMAN CAPOTE

"Once a man's fifty,
he's entitled only to make large and serious
mistakes. . . . If I had the sense that God gave Truman Capote,
Gore Vidal, Saul Bellow, John Updike, I might have done something
elegant and standoffish. . . . Instead I plunged. I'm tired of
being the most famous unpaid comic in American life."

NORMAN MAILER ON HIS BOOK *MARILYN*

"He meant that I would come to understand that
fiction is more enduring than fact, and that history books are full of it."

WILLIAM BURROUGHS, DISCUSSING JACK KEROUAC'S FICTION

"You have to work with people, whatever assholes they might be."

RAQUEL WELCH ON PROFESSIONALISM

"Don't ask me any questions about
what I want to do. I hate life, I hate making movies, I hate everything.
I hate journalists, I hate everybody."

VIVA, STAR OF ANDY WARHOL FILMS

"My ultimate goal was a long, long film
with everybody in the world smiling and I needed the cooperation
of world governments."

YOKO ONO, TALKING ABOUT FILMMAKING

"Maybe I'll be a corporation executive. . . .
I kinda like the image. Big office. Secretary. . . ."

JIM MORRISON, SPECULATING ON A CAREER CHANGE

"I can't write something
unless it has mystery for me. And the Rolling Stones thing
had no mystery."

TRUMAN CAPOTE ON THE ARTICLE HE WAS SUPPOSED TO WRITE
AFTER HIS TOUR WITH THE STONES

"You gotta keep changing. Shirts, old ladies, whatever."

NEIL YOUNG ON CHANGES IN HIS MUSIC AND HIS LIFE

"If I was trained, I would write really good
things that I can't write. I could write a symphony."

MICK JAGGER

"A lot of people feel that music represents the good life, the
cool world . . . It fills people with vague images of some girls walking along
the beach with their boyfriends, their hair blowing in the wind—what
Clairol is doing. That's Madison Avenue foolishness. I think it fits
fourteen years of age just fine."

ART GARFUNKEL

PETE SEEGER/photo by Herbert Wise

"The hard part is keeping your own instincts alive.
Your internal detector, your shit detector, has to switch into higher gear."

ROBIN WILLIAMS ON FAME

"What you're reaching for is never
what you get. Einstein was mathematically trying to prove
the existence of God. He winds up with the theory of relativity."

DUSTIN HOFFMAN

"I'd like to publish a political, spiritual,
and emotional publication or . . . open a restaurant."

JERRY RUBIN, 1977

"I considered preaching, but
preachers don't make a lot and they have to work hard."

WILLIE NELSON

"I ain't gonna play in no coat. Why,
a coat on a pool player is like ice cream on a hot dog."

MINNESOTA FATS

"Do you know the difference between
education and experience? Education is when you read the fine print;
experience is what you get when you don't."

PETE SEEGER

"I'd rather be a Ranger than president of the United States."

A.Y. ALLEE, TEXAS RANGERS CAPTAIN

"The whole point of doing work
is to communicate . . . and the album includes on it fuck, piss, shit,
seed, nigger—it's got everything but shitlicker on it. . . . We're
communicating to a lot of people."

PATTI SMITH ON *EASTER*

"What I fear, far more than selling out, is wearing out."

NORMAN MAILER

"There is only one job I would take after I retire
from this department and that is Justice of the Supreme Court."

ED DAVIS, LOS ANGELES POLICE CHIEF

"I always love the smell of a bat and a glove,
or a hockey puck in the wintertime. Everything I do is according to
baseball . . . and I picked the Toronto Maple Leaf team because
the name is just like nature."

TINY TIM, A SPORTS FAN, ON HIS FAVORITE TEAM

"There are two things
we don't talk about: our sex lives and our contracts."

GORDIE HOWE, AFTER HE AND HIS TWO SONS SIGNED WITH THE
NEW ENGLAND WHALERS HOCKEY TEAM IN 1977

"You can say a pump is as good as coming with a chick in bed."

ARNOLD SCHWARZENEGGER ON "PUMPING UP"

"Fighters are just brutes
who come to entertain the rich white people. The masters
get two of us big black slaves and let us fight it out while they bet,
'My slave can whup your slave.' "

CASSIUS CLAY IN 1964

"After the fight is over and Frazier don't answer
the bell, I'm gonna jump over the ropes and I'm gonna whup Howard Cosell."

MUHAMMAD ALI

"It reminds me of something that happened
in the past. It was two days after the bomb was dropped
at Hiroshima. I was there, and the feeling I had then is the same way I
feel today about O. J.'s injury."

RALPH WILSON, OWNER OF THE BUFFALO BILLS, DISCUSSING O. J. SIMPSON

"A lot of people would like to imply
we're the victims of a permissive society.
Well, I'll tell you this. We don't have one player on my team who does
his own thing. At Ohio State they do *our* thing."

WOODY HAYES, OHIO STATE UNIVERSITY FOOTBALL COACH, 1973

"When they operated on my arm,
I asked them to put in a Koufax fastball. They did, but
it was a Mrs. Koufax fastball."

TOMMY JOHN, DODGER PITCHER

"If somebody comes to me and says,
'. . . I'm stronger than you are, and I have bigger arms than you,
but I want them to be much bigger. . . . How do I do it?'—then he can
be 100 percent sure that I will fuck him up."

WEIGHT LIFTER ARNOLD SCHWARZENEGGER

"When I was hitting in nineteen straight,
I had to listen to 'Boogie Oogie Oogie' every day, because I heard it
on the radio the first day of the streak."

JERRY REMY OF THE BOSTON RED SOX GIVING THE SECRET OF HIS SUCCESS

"Who the hell wants to see a lot of broads,
half-dressed, jumping around like ninnies?"

HAROLD BALLARD, OWNER OF THE HAMILTON, CANADA, TIGER-CATS,
ON CHEERLEADERS

"I've often thought of the fame of football
as just one big *Let's Make a Deal*. Pete Rozelle is Monty Hall,
and the rest of us are a bunch of guys dressed up like radishes or
carrots or other idiot-type things."

MIKE ADAMLE, CHICAGO BEARS

"It is an honor to be associated with a group
whose won-and-lost record was certainly better than my own."

HENRY KISSINGER ON BEING NAMED AN HONORARY MEMBER
OF THE HARLEM GLOBETROTTERS

"I epitomize America."

JOHN DENVER

"Most ballplayers like music they can hit to
or fuck to; I was into more lyrical things."

EX-RED SOX PITCHER BILL "THE SPACEMAN" LEE ON WARREN ZEVON'S MUSIC

"I'm—along with the Queen, you know—
one of the best things England's got. Me and the Queen."

MICK JAGGER

"In my heart I feel Mexican-German.
I feel if I were to organize it correctly, I would try to sing like a Mexican
and think like a German. I get it mixed up sometimes anyway. I sing
like a Nazi and I think like a Mexican and I can't get
anything right."

LINDA RONSTADT

"I'm in my thirties; I'm not only part
of the establishment, I am the establishment."

PETE TOWNSHEND

"You know, there's something about me
that makes a lot of people want to throw up."

PAT BOONE

"I'm like the cockroach in the sink.
Put on the hot water and he'll go down the drain, but sooner or later,
he'll go back up again."

FREDDIE FENDER ON HIS CAREER

"It reminds me of pie crust.
I was always told that flakiness was a desirable quality, not a vice."

JERRY BROWN, RESPONDING TO CRITICISM THAT HE IS "FLAKY"

"The image we have, it would be
impossible for Mickey Mouse to maintain. We're just . . . normal people."

KAREN CARPENTER ON THE CARPENTERS' "WHOLESOME" IMAGE

"What really pleases me
is that I've turned out to be like—
you know that old line—the person my parents warned me about."

KEN GAUL, DIRECTOR OF THE NEW YORK EROTIC FILM FESTIVAL

"I'm the type of guy who'd sell you a rat's asshole for a wedding ring."

TOM WAITS

"Some people like to raise flowers; I like to raise hell."

REPRESENTATIVE BARBARA A. MIKULSKI

"I am a sensitive writer, actor, and director.
Talking business disgusts me. If you want to talk business, call
my disgusting personal manager."

SYLVESTER STALLONE'S CARD, WHICH HE HANDS OUT WHEN APPROACHED
WITH BUSINESS PROPOSITIONS

"I was the onliest boxer in history people asked questions like a senator."

MUHAMMAD ALI

"It's very easy to presume that I'm not a human being."

FRANK ZAPPA

"I'm more famous in the poultry business than show business."

ALICE COOPER, WHO WAS INCORRECTLY RUMORED TO HAVE BITTEN A LIVE
CHICKEN'S HEAD OFF ONSTAGE

"I'm going to be the new J. Edgar Hoover
of Washington. He used to know where all the dirt in Washington was,
but now I'm the one who does."

A. J. WEBERMAN, WHO ANALYZED THE CONTENTS OF
SPIRO AGNEW'S TRASH CANS

"Ah'm not as good
as ah once was, but ah'm as good once as ah ever was."

RONNIE HAWKINS

"I have a New York code of ethics.
Speak unto others as you would have them speak unto you.
In other words, watch your mouth."

LOU REED ON HIS SCUFFLE WITH DAVID BOWIE

"Anything anybody said I did after nine o'clock at night is probably true."

GRACE SLICK ON HER ROWDY BEHAVIOR

"I am like Che Guevara, except I'm doing it in a TV series."

ACTOR DAVID CARRADINE ON HIS ROLE IN *KUNG FU*

"I suppose to most people I'm probably seen
as an amiable idiot—a genial twit. I'm a victim of me own practical jokes."

KEITH MOON

"When I was young, we read the Bible and UFO magazines.
Just like I say I'm equal parts Balenciaga and Brando, well my dad was
equal parts God and Hagar the Spaceman in Mega City. My mother
taught me fantasy; my mother's like a real hip Scheherazade.
Between the two of 'em, I developed a sensibility."

PATTI SMITH

"I was a wise-ass in school,
pretty much equal parts wise and ass."

RICHARD "CHEECH" MARIN OF CHEECH AND CHONG

"In high school I was unanimously voted
least likely to succeed. It took a lot of pressure off me to do anything."

GEORGE THOROGOOD OF GEORGE THOROGOOD AND THE DESTROYERS

"If I, at San Mateo High School, had been told
that the Boy Watchers were gonna rate me above everybody else, I'da said,
'Hoss, you been sniffing that glue.' "

KRIS KRISTOFFERSON'S COMMENT ON BEING NAMED NUMBER ONE ON
THE BOY WATCHER'S ANNUAL LIST

"My teeth—I don't like the way they protrude.
I'm going to have them done but I just haven't had the time. Apart from
that, I'm perfect."

FREDDIE MERCURY OF QUEEN

"Everyone looks tall and fat next to me."

GRAHAM PARKER, FIVE FOOT FIVE

"My friends tell me I keep getting handsomer the older
I get. I have no doubt that's true. I had nowhere to go but up."

DUSTIN HOFFMAN

"I think of myself as an intelligent,
sensitive human with the soul of a clown, which always forces me
to blow it at the most important moments."

JIM MORRISON

"In a word, I'm boring."

RANDY NEWMAN

"My mother speaks to me once every two years
and asks me when I'm going to open a drugstore."

WOODY ALLEN

"The only reason I'm known in Turkey
is because I'm supposed to have gone out with Mrs. Trudeau."

MICK JAGGER

"My image has been the wholesome
girl-next-door, apple-cheek-Annie thing, and I want you people to know
that under these clothes and behind this façade, this body is a mass
of hickeys."

ANNE MURRAY

"I'm very fascinated with the whole
concept of the geisha. They could do everything to perfection. I'm only
a half-assed geisha. I can only sing."

LINDA RONSTADT

"Like Ford was the founder of Ford,
Edison the founder of electricity, Bell was the telephone, I'm the founder
of rock & roll. So if I'm the founder, then I'm the king of it."

LITTLE RICHARD

"I've never flipped out; I'm too crazy to flip out."

VAN MORRISON ON THE PRESSURES OF THE MUSIC BUSINESS

"I have tried to become conservative.
In 1958 I resolved to be simply a piano player. That was the year
I lost $800,000."

LIBERACE

"The movies lie. They lie about women;
they lie about third world people; they make women or blacks look silly."

JANE FONDA

BRUCE JENNER, VALERIE PERRINE, JANE FONDA AND THE VILLAGE PEOPLE/photo by UPI

"We want to be the Bob Hopes of the doper generation."

TOMMY CHONG OF CHEECH AND CHONG

"We are not the Steve and Eydie of our generation."

KRIS KRISTOFFERSON ON HIMSELF AND WIFE RITA COOLIDGE

"I've always wanted to be Jesus;
let's face it, any Irishman has. A lot of my humor is like
Christ coming down from the cross—it has no meaning until much later on."

MICHAEL O'DONOGHUE

"I am totally the product of my own desires. I have life dicked."

TED NUGENT

"I never needed Panavision
and stereophonic sound to woo the world. I did it in black and white
on a screen the size of a postage stamp. Honey, that's talent."

MAE WEST

"There are two kinds of people in the world.
There are the overtly talented and those who are not. I belong
in the former category."

LIVINGSTON TAYLOR

"I'm a perfectionist. . . . People think I'm probably one of those who lounge around, but I'm always on my knees—I do my own floors 'cause no one can please me."

TINA TURNER

"Nobody does Lou Reed better than Lou Reed, man. And don't you ever fucking forget it."

LOU REED

"I was never really interested in becoming a star. I'd dreamed all my life of becoming a stewardess."

GWEN DICKEY, LEAD SINGER FOR ROSE ROYCE

"I don't think of myself as a star. I didn't set out to become a star—I set out to become a singer. The star part is just something that they made up in Hollywood in 1930."

LINDA RONSTADT

"I never considered myself the greatest, but I'm the best."

JERRY LEE LEWIS

"I never wanted to be famous, but I always wanted to be great."

RAY CHARLES

"I guess if you wanted to, you could
call me a millionaire. I wouldn't say that. I figure I got
everything it takes me to live. I got a home that's paid for, hell,
and my kids are straight for the rest of their lives. I got a
little studio here that I can do my work in. Well, you know, I got a car, a
couple of airplanes. What the hell more do you want? Shit, you
can sleep in but one bed at a time. And according to the law,
you ain't supposed to have but one woman at a time or
at least under the same conditions. So I got
everything I need."

RAY CHARLES ON BEING A MILLIONAIRE

"There's fame and there's fortune.
I try to get the fortune, 'cause that's what you can spend."

J. J. CALE

"It means that you have,
as performers will call it, 'fuck you' money. . . .
All that means is that I don't have to do what I don't want to do."

JOHNNY CARSON ON SUCCESS

"I've been in trouble all of my life;
I've done the most unutterable rubbish,
all because of money. I didn't need it. . . . The lure of
the zeros was simply too great."

RICHARD BURTON

"Money will never make you happy, and happy will never make you money."

JIMMY DESTRI OF BLONDIE ON SUCCESS

"What am I supposed to do with the money I earn? Give it back?"

ROD STEWART, RESPONDING TO CRITICISM OF HIS WEALTH
BY THE BRITISH PUNK BANDS

"I worked for charity all my life, and
now it's kind of fun to work for money."

CHARLOTTE FORD

"If I seem to be the new Messiah, fantastic.
My aim is to make a big pile and get out while the going is good."

NICK LOWE

"If you come to get it, get it.
Like the Incas did to the conquistadores—
when the Spaniards came for the Incas' gold, the Incas
pried open the Spaniards' mouths and poured 'em full of all the
molten gold they could fuckin' hold."

ROBERT MITCHUM

"I tell you, water is more valuable than gold or women."

A CALIFORNIA FARMER

"Why you know me. Gimme loose fittin'
shoes, a taght pussy and a warm place to shit and I'm fahn."

WRITER TERRY SOUTHERN, QUOTING ACTOR SLIM PICKENS

"I'll tell you what coloreds want.
It's three things: first, a tight pussy; second, loose
shoes; and third, a warm place to shit. That's all!"

EARL BUTZ, SECRETARY OF AGRICULTURE IN 1976

"I don't think many of the black people
in the U.S. even look on Andy Young as a black man.
Have you ever seen him? He's not very black."

BARRY GOLDWATER, SPEAKING IN SOUTH AFRICA

"It's great when they're little pickaninnies;
they're cute and everybody's a do-gooder. But what about
when they're older . . . fourteen or fifteen?"

WILLIAM POTTER, A PENNSYLVANIA JUDGE, RULING NONWHITE
CHILDREN COULD NOT BE ADOPTED BY WHITE PARENTS

"They don't believe in the same sort
of entertainment as we do. Blacks do war dances, etc."

SYBRAND VAN NIEKERK, SOUTH AFRICAN OFFICIAL

"Our view repeatedly expressed was that
the most practical solution would be to shepherd the
aborigines to an offshore island and bomb them."

FROM A REPORT BY THE AUSTRALIAN COMMUNITY RELATIONS
BUREAU ON RACIAL DISCRIMINATION

"If I shot a black in Australia
or New Zealand or anywhere else in the world, they'd put me in jail for
twenty years. Here I can do it legally."

AN AMERICAN MERCENARY IN RHODESIA

"More white people were fatally shot
by police officers last year than black people [in Los Angeles].
So we don't discriminate."

ED DAVIS, CHIEF OF THE LOS ANGELES POLICE DEPARTMENT, 1975

"I read in the encyclopedia
that Ghana exports most of the world's cocoa. I just love chocolate."

SHIRLEY TEMPLE BLACK, AMBASSADOR TO GHANA, 1974

"I've been called that all my life. All I hope is that he buys my next album."

JAMES BROWN, RESPONDING TO BEING CALLED A "JIVE-ASS NIGGER"
BY ELVIS COSTELLO

"We are built a little differently,
built for speed—skinny calves, long legs, high asses
are all characteristics of blacks. That's why blacks wear
long socks. We have skinny calves and short socks
won't stay up."

O. J. SIMPSON

"I'm patient for thirty, forty, fifty or so years.
After that I'm gone. If it happens in my time—hooray, you know?"

MARVIN GAYE ON RACIAL EQUALITY

"I'm black; you can see it. I don't
have to wear a big wooly head of hair. I like straight hair, I wear it,
I feel myself; you don't see me walking around trying to be white."

TINA TURNER BEING CRITICIZED FOR NOT WEARING AN AFRO

"They asked me what I thought of
black power. I said black power is me making it with Aretha Franklin."

BLUESMAN JUNIOR WELLS

"Everybody's colored or else you wouldn't be able to see them."

CAPTAIN BEEFHEART

"No Vietcong ever called me 'nigger.' "

MUHAMMAD ALI, WHEN HE REFUSED TO BE DRAFTED IN 1967

"You white folks sick enough to believe
you can still draft niggers into your army and send 'em down
to Fort Benning, Georgia, and teach 'em to be guerrillas and send 'em to
Vietnam killin' foreigners to liberate foreigners and think they not gonna
come back to America and kill you to liberate their mammy?"

COMEDIAN DICK GREGORY

"I've been into many [ghettos] and,
to some extent, I'd have to say this:
If you've seen one city slum, you've seen them all."

SPIRO AGNEW

"I wrote a song about Africa
because in Africa the animals are animals.
The tiger is a tiger, the snake is a snake; you know
what the hell he's gonna do. Here in New York, the asphalt jungle,
a tiger or a snake may come up looking like you."

SLY STONE

"In New York the Sex Pistols wouldn't
survive five minutes, man. The Puerto Ricans
would jack 'em right off; they'd say, 'What is this shit?
What are these pins in your ears?' . . . They think they're starvin';
put 'em up on 117th Street and let them check
that neighborhood."

WILLY DeVILLE, LEADER OF MINK DeVILLE, DOWN ON PUNKS

"Will the delegates be issued guns?"

ANN JORDAN, DEMOCRATIC NATIONAL COMMITTEE MEMBER, ON THE
POSSIBILITY OF HOLDING THE 1976 DEMOCRATIC CONVENTION
IN NEW YORK

"Members of Congress have been spending
more money than they have, just like New York City. . . . The only
difference is that Congress can print money and New York can't."

VICE PRESIDENT NELSON ROCKEFELLER, IN 1976

"Guilt feelings have plagued us all.
We knew it was a bad investment when we sold it."

INDIAN LEADERS RESPONDING TO NEW YORK CITY'S THREATENED BANKRUPTCY
WITH AN OFFER TO BUY BACK THE LAND FOR $24

"This muck heaves and palpitates. It is multidirectional
and has a mayor."

AUTHOR DONALD BARTHELME ON NEW YORK CITY

"You have to be a little bit crazy to live in New York."

BELLA ABZUG IN 1977

"New York is like a Wild West town now.
You can pick up a newspaper and see people being held hostage
in a sporting goods store in Brooklyn."

ANDY WARHOL

"New York is a much better place to buy a thrill.
Compared to New York, this place is like living in the morgue.
L.A. is marked by excesses of every kind and complete disregard for
humanity, as if it were built for the automobile and for
hamburger stand operators."

WALKER BECKER OF STEELY DAN ON LIFE IN LOS ANGELES

"Sometimes I get bored riding down the
beautiful streets of L.A. I know it sounds crazy, but I just want to go
to New York and see people . . . suffer."

DONNA SUMMER

"L.A. is a meat factory
that grinds people into neat little packages. I didn't want to be
a neat little package."

KEITH MOON, EXPLAINING WHY HE LEFT

**"Yes, I think the phone has
reached down there. They even have indoor toilets."**

RON NESSEN, BRIEFING REPORTERS PRIOR TO PRESIDENT FORD'S VISIT
TO ELKINS, WEST VIRGINIA

🌿

**"It's been 112 years since we
burned Atlanta, and maybe it's time we did it again."**

A NORTHERN POLITICAL OPERATIVE FOR CARTER, COMPLAINING OF CAMPAIGN
DECISION MAKERS IN ATLANTA

🌿

**"Chicago still reminds me of
Mussolini's Italy. I consider Richard Daley basically a fascist, and the
town is sort of run that way. If you tangle with the boss, you get
castor oil poured down your throat."**

CARTOONIST BILL MAULDIN IN 1976

🌿

**"I'd really like to travel again—
anywhere but Italy. There's too much kidnapping there."**

PATTY HEARST

🌿

"Us Italians brought culture to America."

FRANK RIZZO, MAYOR OF PHILADELPHIA, 1971

🌿

**"When Brutus gave it to him [Caesar] in the back
with that knife, you know if Brutus'd had a gun they would have talked
about gun control. But they didn't put in knife control
or we'd all have to be eating spaghetti all the time."**

ED DAVIS, LOS ANGELES POLICE CHIEF, 1975

"In Brazil the present generation didn't receive
any political or social education. So we provide them with a mechanism
for protest; it is a protest through consumption."

ROBERT ORSI OF PEPSI COLA, WHOSE SALES SLOGAN IN BRAZIL
IS "THE PEPSI REVOLUTION"

"Brazil can become the importer of pollution. . . . We have
a lot left to pollute. And if we don't do it, some other country will."

JOÃO VELLOSO, BRAZIL'S PLANNING MINISTER, 1972

"I always wanted to come to Germany.
I always knew I wanted to come here, just like some guys always knew
they wanted to wear a dress."

IGGY POP ON BERLIN

"Switzerland is my favorite place now,
because it's so—nothing. There's absolutely nothing to do."

ANDY WARHOL

"You can't have a little bit of autonomy
any more than you can be a little bit pregnant. Either we run our own
affairs or we don't."

BOB ERLAM, RESIDENT OF THE YUKON, PROTESTING THAT CANADA CONTINUES
TO RUN THE YUKON LIKE A COLONY

"The spirit of the British is, was, and
always will be 99.9 percent proof. American spirit is about 80 percent
proof, because Americans are never sure whether or not they're
going to pull through."

NICHOLAS SOAMES, WINSTON CHURCHILL'S GRANDSON

"This is a very horrible country, England.
We invented the mackintosh, you know. We invented the flasher, the
voyeur. That's what the press is about."

MALCOLM McLAREN, PUNK ROCK MANAGER

"I think you have a cute little country."

RANDY NEWMAN TO AN INTERVIEWER IN ENGLAND

"Some of these people are not too far removed
from the wild tribes of the district of the inner mountains
of Mexico. I don't think you can throw the genes out of the question
when you discuss future behavior patterns of people."

BILL PARKER, LOS ANGELES POLICE CHIEF FROM 1950 TO 1966, TALKING ABOUT
THAT AREA'S MEXICAN-AMERICAN COMMUNITY

"Southern people just don't know Jews;
all they know is niggers. They regard Jews like Chinese; give 'em enough
rope and they'll start a rope factory."

KINKY FRIEDMAN

"The French are just useless. They can't organize a piss-up in a brewery."

ELTON JOHN

"In the heroin business
the Mexicans are the short-order cooks. The French are the chefs."

STERLING JOHNSON, NEW YORK CITY SPECIAL NARCOTICS PROSECUTOR

"Metric is definitely communist.
One monetary system, one language, one weight and measurement
system, one world—all communist! We know the West was won
by the inch, foot, yard, and mile."

DEAN KRAKEL, DIRECTOR OF THE NATIONAL
COWBOY HALL OF FAME

"Our students don't need complete fluency.
Even if you go abroad now, you don't need a language.
The dollar speaks louder than anything."

JAMES T. GUINES, WASHINGTON ELEMENTARY-SCHOOL DEPUTY SUPERINTENDENT,
DISCUSSING FOREIGN-LANGUAGE TEACHERS, IN 1977

"The torch of Western civilization is being carried
solely by America. The psychotic thing is all over here. We got the
white man's burden."

JERRY CASALE, BASS PLAYER FOR DEVO

"We should keep the Panama Canal. After all, we stole it fair and square."

SENATOR S. I. HAYAKAWA

"My uncle Teddy stole it,
my father Franklin kept it going, and as far as I'm concerned,
they can now give it back."

JAMES ROOSEVELT ON THE PANAMA CANAL

"When Africans have a man to lunch, they really have him to lunch."

RONALD REAGAN, WHILE GOVERNOR OF CALIFORNIA

"We had nothing to do
with Chile or Allende. That was the Chileans."

RICHARD NIXON

🍃

"The CIA was instructed by President Nixon
to play a direct role in organizing a military coup d'etat in Chile
to prevent Allende's accession to the presidency."

1976 REPORT FROM THE SENATE SELECT COMMITTEE ON INTELLIGENCE

🍃

"I was a hippie, and everything was beautiful and
I loved Negroes and everything. I'd been sheltered; I wasn't out in the
cold world. Now, hell—I'd vote for George Wallace tomorrow if he was
runnin' for president. I hope we get a little more aggressive and start
telling these pea-pickin' little countries that they
can't shove us around anymore."

STEVE WALSH OF THE ROCK GROUP KANSAS

🍃

"From the air, Thailand looks like a cantaloupe convention."

BOB HOPE, REFERRING TO THE SHAVEN HEADS OF MONKS

🍃

"It's almost as good as having the president.
Rockefeller's name is known everywhere. He's a symbol of America."

U.S. OFFICIAL ON VICE PRESIDENT NELSON ROCKEFELLER'S
1975 VISIT TO TAIWAN

🍃

"There is no real proof that the Holocaust actually did happen."

GEORGE PAPE, PRESIDENT OF THE GERMAN-AMERICAN COMMITTEE OF
GREATER NEW YORK, OBJECTING TO THE HOLOCAUST CURRICULUM
IN NEW YORK CITY SCHOOLS

"They were gooks, they were dinks,
they were slants. We hated the whole people. They were ugly.
They chewed betel nuts. They ate lice out of each other's hair. It was
always 'Blow 'em away.' "

VETERAN KENNETH CAMPBELL, TESTIFYING BEFORE AN AD HOC CONGRESSIONAL
PANEL ON WAR CRIMES

"We should have bombed
the hell out of them the minute we got into office."

HENRY KISSINGER, A WEEK AFTER THE 1973 VIETNAM PEACE AGREEMENT

"Those who remained honest were considered crazy."

VIETNAMESE GENERAL LU LAN, SPEAKING IN 1975 ON CORRUPTION IN SAIGON

"The main point arises from the fact
that I've always acted alone; Americans like that
immensely. Americans like the cowboy who leads the wagon train by
riding ahead alone on his horse, the cowboy who rides all alone into the
town, the village, with his horse and nothing else. Maybe without a
pistol, since he doesn't shoot. He acts, that's all, by being in
the right place at the right time. In short, a Western."

HENRY KISSINGER

"I've seen Europe on television
and thousands of Europeans, so really it was nothing new to me.
You can learn as much about going abroad by watching and reading news
and reading books and stories and publications as you can by seeing some
concrete walls, a few automobiles in traffic jams, and some scenery."

GEORGE WALLACE, COMMENTING ON HIS FIRST TRIP TO EUROPE

"I understand there are Arabs who are not dirty."

PAUL RAND DIXON, FEDERAL TRADE COMMISSIONER IN 1977, REPLYING TO A
REQUEST TO RETRACT A RACIAL SLUR DIRECTED AT RALPH NADER

"They want to buy oranges from Florida.
They want to buy wheat from Kansas, and who knows, they may want to
pick up New York City's debt."

REPRESENTATIVE PIERRE S. DuPONT ON SAUDI ARABIA

"This is beautiful. I've always wanted to see the Persian Gulf."

SENATOR WILLIAM SCOTT TO EGYPTIAN PRESIDENT ANWAR SADAT
WHILE OVERLOOKING THE SUEZ CANAL

"What's this Gaza stuff? I never have understood that."

SENATOR WILLIAM SCOTT TO ISRAELI PRIME MINISTER ITZHAK RABIN

"What a terrible revenge for Pearl Harbor."

S. I. HAYAKAWA ON THE SUCCESS OF McDONALD'S HAMBURGERS IN JAPAN

"Tell them Nips I've never read anything about me
from Japan that wasn't disgusting bullshit. . . . I love the way
them Nips talk in hieroglyphics."

TED NUGENT, TALKING TO JAPANESE JOURNALISTS THROUGH AN INTERPRETER

"It is true that I enjoyed my celebrity status
in my previous position, but I can prove that when I left Washington
I wore exactly the same size crown as when I arrived."

HENRY KISSINGER

"I find that professors, like politicians,
should quit while they are ahead—or think they are. Just look at Nixon."

JOHN KENNETH GALBRAITH, ANNOUNCING HIS RETIREMENT IN 1974

"Retirement at sixty-five is ridiculous.
When I was sixty-five, I still had pimples."

GEORGE BURNS

"The only thing good about it is you're not dead."

LILLIAN HELLMAN ON AGING

"I told Dale, 'When I go, just skin me
and put me on top of Trigger.' And Dale said, 'Now don't
get any ideas about me.' "

ROY ROGERS

"Don't worry about when you're going to die,
because you ain't never . . . seen a hearse . . . with luggage on the top."

BELL RECORDING ARTIST GIDEON DANIELS

"It was a very Woody Allen-type
suicide attempt. I turned on all the gas and left the windows open."

ELTON JOHN, TALKING ABOUT HIS REACTION TO BREAKING OFF HIS ENGAGEMENT
TO A MILLIONAIRE HEIRESS

"Fourteen heart attacks,
and he had to die in my week. In *my* week."

JANIS JOPLIN, WHOSE COVER PHOTO ON *NEWSWEEK* WAS PREEMPTED
BY EISENHOWER'S DEATH

"Makes you feel sad, doesn't it? Like your grandfather died. . . .
Yeah, it's just too bad it couldn't have been Mick Jagger."

PUNK ROCK MANAGER MALCOLM McLAREN'S REACTION TO ELVIS' DEATH

"Fuckin' good riddance to bad rubbish.
I don't give a fuckin' shit, and nobody else does either. It's just fun to
fake sympathy, that's all they're doin'."

JOHNNY ROTTEN ON ELVIS' DEATH

"I'm alive and well, but if I were dead I would be the last to know."

PAUL McCARTNEY ON RUMORS OF HIS DEATH

"I have no views.
When one is retired, it's sensible to refrain from having views."

COLUMNIST JOSEPH ALSOP